Korean Banchan Recipes

100 Authentic Side Dishes

from **Japchae** and **Jeon**
to **Kimchi** and **Namul**

Nobuko Kitasaka

TUTTLE Publishing

Tokyo | Rutland, Vermont | Singapore

Contents

South Korea's Make-ahead Banchan Side Dishes 6

Serve Banchan for Simple Everyday Meals 9

Serve on Top of Rice as Bibimbap 10

Banchan to Accompany Your Evening Drinks 11

Korean Ingredients and Seasonings 12

PART 1 Basic Banchan

Jangajji Pickles

Perilla Leaves Marinated in Seasoned Soy Sauce 15

Soy Sauce Jangajji
  Onion Jangajji 17
  King Oyster Mushroom Jangajji 17
  Lotus Root Jangajji 17
  Soybean Jangajji 17
  Mountain Yam Jangajji 17
  Shredded Daikon Jangajji 17

Miso Jangajji
  Myoga Ginger Bud Jangajji 19
  Burdock Root Jangajji 19
  Shishito Pepper Jangajji 19
  Bamboo Shoot Jangajji 19
  Celery Jangajji 19
  Dried Apricot Jangajji 19

Whole Garlic Jangajji 20

How to Enjoy Jangajji 21

Quick and Easy Mixed Banchan

Sliced Pork with Perilla Leaves 22

Garlic Chives and Chicken Tenders with Spicy Sesame Sauce 23

Mixed Semi-dried Fish and Bean Sprouts 24

Spicy Mixed Sashimi and Aromatic Vegetables 25

Spicy Mixed Octopus and Spinach 26

Boiled Squid and Green Onions with Spicy Sauce 26

Cucumber with Gochujang 28

Root Vegetables with Perilla 28

Spicy Daikon Radish 28

Steamed Garlic Chives with Roasted Soybean Powder 30

Mixed Eggplant and Myoga Ginger 31

Mixed Broccoli and Shiitake Mushrooms 31

Nori Seaweed with Yangnyeom Sauce 33

Sliced Zucchini with Walnuts 33

Namul Vegetable Side Dishes

Simple Namuls
Eggplant and Eggplant Skin Namul 35
Bean Sprout Namul 35
Okra Namul 35
Carrot Namul 35

Soy Sauce Namuls
Garlic Chive Namul 37
Mushroom Namul 37
Wakame Seaweed Namul 37
Saltwort Namul 37

Soy Sauce and Doenjang Namuls
Bitter Gourd Namul 39
Water Celery Namul 39
Broccoli Namul 39
Komatsuna Greens Namul 39

Gochujang Namuls
Hijiki Seaweed Namul 41
Japanese Leek Namul 41
Wood Ear Mushroom Namul 41
Aralia Erata Shoot Namul 41

Kimchis

Instant Napa Cabbage Kimchi 43

Three Kinds of Instant Kimchi
Cherry Tomato Kimchi 44
Daikon Radish Kimchi 44
Bashed Cucumber Kimchi 44

Chopped Napa Cabbage Kimchi with Yuzu 45

Rolled Napa Cabbage Kimchi 46

Water Kimchi with Citrus 47

Daikon Radish Water Kimchi 48

PART 2 Side Dishes and Main Dishes

Stir-fries

Beef Bulgogi 51

Pork Belly with Gochujang 52

Stir-fried Beef with Shishito Peppers and Garlic 54

Pork and Kimchi Stir-fry 55

Sweet and Spicy Chicken with Gochujang 56

Aromatic Stir-fried Chicken Gizzards 57

Asparagus and Onion Summer Japchae 58

Mushroom Autumn Japchae 59

Kombu Seaweed with Garlic and Soy 61

Sweet and Spicy Sakura Shrimp with Garlic Shoots 61

Eggplant and Onion with Fragrant Miso 62

Spicy Konnyaku Stir-fry 63

Sweet and Spicy Baby Anchovies with Nuts 65

Stewed and Simmered Dishes

Simmered Chicken and Soybeans 67

Sweet and Spicy Chicken Drumettes 68

Glazed Pork and Green Onion Rolls 69

Stewed Meat-stuffed Eggplant 70

Beef and Eggs Simmered in Soy 72

Stewed Beef with Taro Root 73

Spicy Simmered Fish with Daikon Radish 75

Spicy Spanish Mackerel Simmered with Potato 76

Korean Style Mackerel Simmered in Miso 77

Tofu Simmered with Kimchi 78

Tofu Simmered with Spicy Cod Roe 78

Spicy Fish Cakes with Onion 80

Sweet and Spicy Boiled Eggs with Walnuts 81

Seasoned Lotus Root 83

Potatoes Simmered with Dried Anchovies 83

A Feast with a Cut of Meat

Seasoned Boiled Pork 85

Pork Simmered with Asian Pear 86

Jeon Pancakes

Flour-based Jeon
Corn and Onion Jeon 89
Shrimp and Chrysanthemum Greens Jeon 89
Napa Cabbage Jeon 89
Beet and Onion Jeon 91
Whitebait and Green Onion Jeon 91
Arugula Jeon 91

Nori Wrapped Enoki Jeon 92

Rice Jeon 93

Shredded Sweet Potato Jeon 94

Stuffed Shiitake Jeon 95

Conventions Used in This Book

1 tablespoon is equal to 15 ml, and 1 teaspoon is equal to 5 ml.

The indicated shelf life is a rough time estimate starting from the point at which the food is placed into a clean storage container, tightly covered, and put in the refrigerator (or freezer). Because food safety depends on temperature and storage conditions, prepared foods should be eaten as soon as possible, particularly during the summer months.

A 600-watt microwave oven has been used to develop these recipes. Please adjust the microwaving times as needed to suit your microwave oven's wattage.

The sugar used is raw cane sugar, and the stock used is dashi stock made with dried anchovies (see below).

How to Make Dried Anchovy Dashi Stock

AN EASY-TO-MAKE AMOUNT

4¼ cups (1 liter) water

⅓ scant cup dried anchovies (myeolchi or niboshi) (about ½ oz / 15 g)

One 4-in (10-cm) square piece dried kombu seaweed

1 teaspoon whole black peppercorns

Vegetable scraps, such as root and stem ends of onions, root ends of green onions (scallions) and the dark green parts of leeks

Put all of the ingredients into a saucepan set over medium heat. Reduce the heat to low once the contents come to a boil, and simmer for about 20 minutes. Strain through a colander.

* If the dried anchovies are large, gut them beforehand. Small anchovies can be used whole.

Perilla Leaves Marinated in Seasoned Soy Sauce ➡ page 15

South Korea's Make-ahead Banchan Side Dishes

When you have a selection of ready-made side dishes stocked in the refrigerator, you can rest assured that daily meal prep will be easy!

Banchan—An Expression of Thoughtfulness

When you enter a Korean restaurant, you will find a variety of side dishes on small plates lined up on the table before the food you have ordered is served. These are *banchan*. In Korean households, it is regarded as considerate of the mother (*eomeoni*) to prepare a variety of side dishes for the family. In K-dramas, a mother is often shown removing various storage containers from the fridge, or serving up multiple side dishes to her family.

Store Them in Airtight Containers in the Refrigerator

While preparing banchan, make enough food to be divided between several meals. Put the leftovers into storage containers with tight-fitting lids and store them in the refrigerator. Glass storage containers that allow one to see their contents have become popular in South Korea.

South Korea's Make-ahead Banchan Side Dishes

Stir-fry, Stew and Jeon Leftovers Can Be Reheated Before Serving

Stir-fried or stewed foods can be reheated in the microwave, or transferred to a pot and warmed up to a simmer if they have a broth. *Jeon* (fritters) can be reheated on both sides in a skillet over medium-low heat, or lightly warmed in a toaster oven. You can quickly prepare meals from leftovers for family members who come home late or for one person.

Serve Banchan for Simple Everyday Meals

With a few banchan on hand, you can set a fine table just by serving them with rice and miso soup. Here, stewed fish is the main dish, supplemented with veggies in the form of *namul* (seasoned cooked vegetables) and kimchi.

Clockwise from top to bottom: **Sliced Zucchini with Walnuts** ➡ page 33
Namuls (Bean Sprouts Namul / Eggplant and Eggplant Skin Namul / Carrot Namul / Komatsuna Greens Namul / Aralia Erata Shoot Namul) ➡ pages 35, 39, 41
Beef and Eggs Simmered in Soy ➡ page 72

Gochujang Sauce ➡ page 52

Serve on Top of Rice as Bibimbap

Put any side dish you like—as much as you like—on hot rice! If you put on various kinds of namul, you can make a *bibimbap* (rice with toppings) with lots of vegetables. If you also add stewed meat and eggs, you will have a meal with perfectly balanced nutrition. Serve with Gochujang Sauce and add a drizzle of sesame oil. Mix well before eating.

Banchan to Accompany Your Evening Drinks

Clockwise from top to bottom:
**Cherry Tomato Kimchi ➡ page 44 Aralia Erata Shoot Namul ➡ page 41
Aromatic Stir-fried Chicken Gizzards ➡ page 57**

Banchan make great snacks to accompany alcoholic beverages. The well-seasoned little dishes with adult flavors make your adult beverages taste even better. The typical drinks you might think of to accompany Korean dishes are beer or *makgeolli* (sparkling rice wine), but I often serve banchan with Japanese sake, or pair red kimchi with red wine.

Mix the Sauce with Noodles

Dishes that use gochujang as the sauce can be mixed with boiled somen noodles to make *bibimmyeon* (spicy mixed noodles). Often, people turn their noses up at leftover salads when the sauce has separated from the other ingredients, but in South Korea, home cooks find this sauce convenient for stirring into dishes like *bibimmyeon*. Garnish with sprouts or red chili peppers.

Spicy Mixed Sashimi and Aromatic Vegetables ➡ page 25

Korean Ingredients and Seasonings

Korean ingredients and seasonings are indispensable to Korean cooking. You can easily obtain these at Korean grocery stores as well as general Asian grocery stores and supermarkets, as well as online. Although I have included notes about foods you can substitute, using the original ingredients will make the flavors much closer to those you would find in South Korea, so I highly recommend that you include them in your banchan-making adventures.

1 Perilla Leaves

Perilla leaves have a uniquely refreshing flavor. Although they are visually very similar to green shiso leaves, they are larger and stiffer, and have a different flavor and aroma. If you wrap stir-fries or grilled meats with perilla leaves, they will leave a fresh aftertaste in your mouth. The Perilla Leaves Marinated in Seasoned Soy Sauce (➡ page 15) can be stored for quite a while, so I encourage you to give it a try!

2 Green Chili Peppers (Raw)

These peppers have a fresh spiciness. They are eaten as-is, minced and added to sauces, and often used in conjunction with ripe red chili peppers. They can be used whole in Miso Jangajji (➡ page 19). It's convenient to freeze them in bulk when they are in season. They can be substituted with shishito peppers or Manganji peppers.

3 Aekjeot (Korean Fish Sauce)

This is an indispensable ingredient in Kimchi Sauce (➡ page 43). The photo shows one made with Pacific sand eel. In South Korea, fish sauce made with sardines is often used too. A little goes a long way, so add it as a background flavor in mixed dishes, or use as a sauce for hotpots. You can substitute *nam pla* (Thai fish sauce) or Japanese fish sauce.

4 Deulgireum (Perilla Oil)

An oil extracted from roasting perilla seeds, this ingredient is indispensable for seasoning namul. Both the flavor and aroma are milder than sesame oil, and in South Korea, it is more commonly used than sesame oil. It is rich in α-linolenic acid and helps to ward off high blood pressure and arteriosclerosis. Dark sesame oil can be substituted.

5 Sesame Oil

Korean sesame oil is characterized by the way that it is darker and stronger in aroma than Japanese sesame oil. Besides using it in fragrant stir-fries, it is brushed onto the *nori* (roasted seaweed) for *kimbap / gimbap* (Korean sushi), or added with salt to boiled pork. It is very Korean to drizzle a little of it on bibimbap for smooth mouthfeel.

6 Deulkkae Garu (Perilla Powder)

A powder derived from roasted and ground perilla seeds. It is said to have antioxidant properties. It has a nutty aroma and sweet taste, and is added to namul, batters and stir-fries. Rich soups with plenty of perilla powder added are popular in South Korea. It can be substituted with ground sesame seeds.

🔟 Doenjang (Korean Miso)
Unlike most types of Japanese miso, Korean doenjang does not incorporate malted grains, but is made only with fermented soybeans. It has a strong fermented aroma similar to Japanese natto, and still has bits of whole soybeans in it. It is used for Soy Sauce and Doenjang Namuls (➡ page 39) as well as stews and soups (*doenjang-jjigae*). You can substitute Japanese miso.

7️⃣ Gochujang
A sweet and spicy miso paste that is made by combining and fermenting mochi rice, ground red chili pepper, rice malt, barley malt, salt and other ingredients. It is not just spicy—it has a deep umami flavor. Besides using it in stews and stir-fries, it is used to flavor bibimbap and namul. The spiciness varies by brand, so find one that suits your taste.

8️⃣ Ground Red Chili Peppers
This versatile seasoning is a powder made from dried and ground red chili peppers. There are coarse and fine grinds; in this book I have used the coarsely ground variety. Korean ground red chili pepper is not overly spicy, and has a subtle sweetness. Use for spicy mixed dishes, stews, sauces and more.

9️⃣ Maesil Chung (Ume or Green Plum Sauce)
When you want to add sweetness, this condiment is used instead of sugar. Added to jangajji sauce or mixed dishes, it imparts the sourness and aroma of the ume and deepens the flavor. I make my own using green ume fruit when they are in season, but you can use a store-bought bottle. If you cannot find it, you can substitute reduced plum wine.

1️⃣1️⃣ Mulyeot (Corn or Brown Rice Syrup)
In Korean cooking, table sugar is not used very often; syrup made from starches such as barley malt is used instead. Korean brands are often made with corn, but I prefer to use a Japanese type that is made from brown rice instead. Honey can be substituted.

1️⃣2️⃣ Saeujeot (Fermented Mysid Shrimp)
This is a fermented product made by preserving small mysid shrimp in salt. It has a lot of umami and richness, and promotes the fermentation of whatever food it is combined with, so it is indispensable for making kimchi. It can also be eaten with boiled pork or used as a seasoning in stews. Japanese brands use bigger shrimp than Korean ones, so I often chop up the shrimp before using it.

1️⃣3️⃣ Daechu (Dried Jujubes)
Jujubes are a fruit used often in Korean as well as Chinese vegan Buddhist cuisine. They promote metabolism and improve elimination problems and anemia, and are said to have cosmetic benefits. They have a subtle sweetness, and are put into soups whole, or chopped and added to kimchi.

Korean Ingredients and Seasonings

PART 1

Basic Banchan

To start with, let me introduce you to easy-to-make banchan. These include: mixed dishes that are convenient to make in large batches, long-keeping Korean pickles called *jangajji*, vegetable-rich namul and instant kimchi, which can be simply made by mixing vegetables. They are indispensable to the Korean dining table. If you make a few of these and have them kept on hand, your dinner table will become very lively!

Jangajji Pickles

Jangajji are Korean pickles. The "jang" in Jangajji stands for soy sauce or miso. Jangajji are made by adding sweetness, sourness or spiciness to the soy sauce or miso and combining this with vegetables to let the flavors permeate. Make several kinds to enjoy a different one every day (see photo ➡ page 5).

Perilla Leaves Marinated in Seasoned Soy Sauce

SHELF LIFE About 2 weeks in the refrigerator

Simply coat perilla leaves with seasoned soy sauce, stack them, and pickle them. Wrapped around rice, the leaves are so delicious, you can't stop eating them! Perilla leaves should be soaked in a 3% salt water solution in advance to allow the flavors to permeate them easier.

AN EASY-TO-MAKE AMOUNT

20 perilla leaves

A ingredients
- 2½ cups (625 ml) water
- 1 tablespoon coarse salt

½ cup (125 ml) Seasoned Soy Sauce (➡ see below)

1 Combine the A ingredients in a bowl and stir to dissolve the salt. Soak the perilla leaves in the salt water for 20 to 30 minutes. Rinse briefly and pat dry.
2 Brush each leaf with the seasoned soy sauce (photo at right) and stack them up in a storage container. They can be eaten after half a day.

Brush each perilla leaf with about 1 teaspoon of the Seasoned Soy Sauce, spread the leaf flat and stack it. Repeat for all the leaves.

NOTE

Seasoned Soy Sauce

It was this amazing sauce that sparked my interest in Korean cuisine. It is versatile enough to be used in salad dressings, stir-fries, and simmered dishes, and is also useful for dipping jeon, topping cold tofu and bibimbap, and as a sauce for pan-fried fish. The spiciness can be adjusted by varying the amount of chili peppers. Part of the appeal of this sauce is that it thickens and more mellow as time goes by. When the amount runs low, you can just add freshly made sauce to it.

SHELF LIFE About 2 weeks in the refrigerator

AN EASY-TO-MAKE AMOUNT

⅓ cup, plus 4 teaspoons (100 ml) soy sauce
⅓ cup, plus 4 teaspoons (100 ml) Dried Anchovy Dashi Stock (➡ page 4)
1 cup (50 g) minced green onions (scallions)
1 teaspoon grated garlic
1 teaspoon ground chili pepper
½ teaspoon sugar
1 teaspoon roasted sesame seeds
Sliced red and green chili peppers, to taste

Combine all the ingredients and mix. Leave to mature at room temperature for half a day to a day, then store in the refrigerator.

Soy Sauce Jangajji

Soy Sauce Jangajji

SHELF LIFE: About 2 weeks in the refrigerator

Refreshing pickled vegetables permeated with a sweet and sour soy sauce flavor. Various textures can be enjoyed depending on the ingredients. They can be used as small appetizers or side dishes; I also recommend chopping them up and using them with *ochazuke* (rice with hot tea or dashi stock), or adding them to fried rice.

AN EASY-TO-MAKE AMOUNT

For the Soy Sauce Brine
- ½ cup (125 ml) light soy sauce
- ½ cup (125 ml) water
- ¼ cup (50 g) sugar
- 1 tablespoon soju, shochu or sake
- 1 tablespoon ume syrup
- ¼ cup (65 ml) rice vinegar

Ingredients of your choice to pickle (see below), to taste (about 5 oz / 150 g)

1 Put all the Soy Sauce Brine ingredients except for the vinegar in a pan over medium heat. When it comes to a boil, add the vinegar and turn off the heat.

2 Put the ingredients to be pickled in a storage container, and pour over the Step-1 brine while it is still hot.

3 Once the contents have cooled, put a lid on the storage container, and leave it to marinate for one day to allow the flavors to permeate.

> If continuing to store beyond 1 week, transfer only the marinade to a small saucepan, bring to a simmer, let cool, and return it to the container. The brine can be refreshed up to three times by bringing it back to a boil each time.

Onion Jangajji

Cut up one small onion into ¾-in (2-cm) dice.

Soybean Jangajji

Use 1 scant cup (about 5 oz / 150 g) of boiled soybeans (➡ page 67). You can also use canned steamed soybeans.

King Oyster Mushroom Jangajji

Slice 3 king oyster mushrooms into ¼-in (6-mm) slices.

Mountain Yam Jangajji

Use 1 cup (about 5 oz / 150 g) of peeled mountain yam (or sweet potato) strips (short lengths sliced about ¼-in / 6-mm thick).

Lotus Root Jangajji

Peel a small lotus root (about 5 oz / 150 g) and slice it into ¼-in (6-mm) rounds. Boil in water with a little vinegar until done to the texture you like.

Shredded Daikon Jangajji

Soak ¼ cup (about 1 oz / 30 g) of dried kiriboshi daikon until softened but firm. Drain well. The photo shows a thickly cut type of kiriboshi daikon.

NOTE

Besides the above, fresh daikon radish, cucumbers, bell peppers, green chili peppers, green tomatoes, Jerusalem artichokes, garlic sprouts (boiled), sansho peppers (boiled) and butterbur (boiled) also work well with this brine. You can also pickle cucumbers and daikon radish, onions and bell peppers, etc. in combination. Other beans, such as green soybeans, work well too.

Miso Jangajji

Miso Jangajji

 SHELF LIFE About 2 weeks in the refrigerator

Sweet barley miso is combined with the slight spiciness that comes from the gochujang red pepper paste. These are rich pickles with the flavors of aromatic vegetables. Omit the miso paste if serving the pickles on their own as appetizers or in *ochazuke* (rice with hot tea or dashi stock), but serve the pickles with the miso paste if eating with plain hot rice.

AN EASY-TO-MAKE AMOUNT

For the miso pickling bed
- 1 cup (250 g) barley miso
- 2 tablespoons gochujang
- ½ tablespoon grated garlic
- 1 tablespoon mulyeot (or honey)
- 2 tablespoons minced green onion (scallions)

1 cup of ingredients of your choice to pickle (see below), to taste (about 5 oz / 150 g)

1 Combine the miso pickling bed ingredients and mix together. Put into a storage container.

2 Bury the vegetable ingredients in the step-1 pickling bed, and pickle from between 30 minutes to up to 2 days.

> If the water exuded by the pickled vegetables comes to the surface of the miso pickling bed, the bed and pickles may become spoiled, so dab it dry occasionally with paper towels.

Myoga Ginger Bud Jangajji

Cut 7 to 8 myoga ginger buds in half if they are large (the flavors from the pickling bed permeate them better if cut), or leave whole if they are smaller.

Bamboo Shoot Jangajji

Cut a small preboiled bamboo shoot into bite-size pieces.

Burdock Root Jangajji

Wash 1 unpeeled burdock root well. Cut diagonally into ¼-in (6-mm) wide pieces. Cook until tender but firm in boiling water with vinegar added.

Celery Jangajji

Remove the leaves and tough strings from a celery stalk, and cut into bite-size pieces. (Celery can also be pickled whole.)

Shishito Pepper Jangajji

Make single lengthwise cuts into 4 to 5 shishito peppers.

Dried Apricot Jangajji

Pickle 3–4 apricots whole. If possible, pickle for about 3 days for plump, tender apricots.

NOTE

You can also pickle two or three kinds of ingredients together at one time, much as you might make *nukazuke* (rice bran pickles). The vegetables can be roughly cut up. Other ingredients that can be pickled in this miso pickling bed include green chilies, Jerusalem artichokes, Peruvian ground apples, Japanese spikenard and garlic (thinly sliced). In addition to dried apricots, sweet foods such as dried persimmons and green ume fruit preserved in syrup also work well with this miso bed.

You can also wrap garlic with meat, fish or vegetables, or use them in salads and mixed dishes as a nice accent.

Whole Garlic Jangajji

 SHELF LIFE About 2 to 3 years at room temperature

After pickling, the odor of the garlic disappears, they become less spicy, and their umami becomes more pronounced. Enjoy them as-is as a snack with tea, or as a small appetizer with alcoholic beverages.

AN EASY-TO-MAKE AMOUNT

2 lbs (1 kg) whole garlic heads

A ingredients
2½ cups (625 ml) rice vinegar
2½ cups (625 ml) water

B ingredients
3 cups (750 ml) pre-pickling liquid (the A ingredient combination)
2 cups (400 g) sugar
½ cup (135 g), plus 1 tablespoon coarse salt

1 cup (250 ml) ume syrup

1 Pre-pickle the garlic. Remove any dirt from the garlic cloves, and peel off most of the skin, leaving one thin inner layer.
2 Place the garlic cloves in a storage container, and add the combined A ingredients. If the garlic cloves are not totally immersed, add more water and rice vinegar in a 1:1 ratio. Close up the container and leave at room temperature for 1 week.
3 Pickle the garlic. Drain the step-2 pre-pickled garlic into a colander (reserve the pickling liquid) and put the garlic back in the storage container.
4 Put the B ingredients in a pan over medium heat and bring to a boil. Leave to cool. Add the ume syrup and mix, and pour the mixture over the step-3 garlic. Close up the storage container and leave at room temperature for at least a month, or for 3 months if possible.

> As time goes by, the garlic becomes softer and less spicy, making it easier to eat. To eat, cut a head in half horizontally and remove one half clove at a time with a fork. You can also peel the garlic cloves in advance and separate them one by one before pickling.

Basic Banchan

How to Enjoy Jangajji

Soy Sauce Jangajji

When Soy Sauce Jangajji (➡ page 17) becomes mature, I recommend chopping it up finely before using. It can be used in *ochazuke* (rice with hot tea or dashi stock), added to fried rice, or used as a filling for rice balls. It can also be spooned over cold tofu with the pickling sauce, or used as a salad dressing.

The pickling liquid can be used as a dipping sauce for *jeon* (fritters), or used to marinate sashimi fish, which is then served on rice as a rice bowl. The sweet-sour sauce works well as a salad dressing too.

Turn soybean jangajji into salad dressing.

Serving jeon with onion jangajji is standard practice.

Miso Jangajji

I often use Miso Jangajji (➡ page 19) chopped up in a miso soup, together with some of the miso pickling bed.

The miso pickling bed gradually becomes more loose and watery the longer you pickle vegetables in it, but the bed is delicious with the flavors of the vegetables permeating it, so it can be used as a paste or sauce on crudités or steamed vegetables, or spread on grilled tofu or rice balls. None of it has to go to waste. It can also be used as a seasoning in stewed or stir-fried dishes, or as a sauce on pan-fried meats or fish.

The miso pickling bed put on boiled pork and wrapped in a leafy vegetable is delicious!

Quick and Easy Mixed Banchan

Mixed dishes can be made quickly with just vegetables, or combined with meat or seafood for a hearty meal. Having a dish like this in your refrigerator gives you peace of mind for dinner preparation.

The rich flavor of the perilla leaves is mixed with pork, which is then seasoned with a spicy sauce to give the dish a kick.

Sliced Pork with Perilla Leaves

 SHELF LIFE — About 3 to 4 days in the refrigerator

SERVES 2 × 2 TIMES

⅙ red onion (1 oz / 30 g)
5 to 6 perilla leaves
1 tablespoon sake
7 oz (200 g) very thinly sliced pork shoulder (cut for shabu shabu)
2 tablespoons Seasoned Soy Sauce (➡ page 15)

1 Thinly slice the red onion, and rip up with perilla leaves with your hands.
2 Bring water to a boil in a pan and add the sake. Spread out the sliced pork and, one by one, put the slices into the boiling water. When the meat changes color, take the slices out of the pan and drain them in a colander.
3 Combine the step-1 and step-2 ingredients in a bowl, add the Seasoned Soy Sauce and mix.

Garlic Chives and Chicken Tenders with Spicy Sesame Sauce

SHELF LIFE — About 3 to 4 days in the refrigerator

The aroma of garlic chives envelops the mild chicken breast. It is a perfect little snack to munch on with that first glass of beer.

SERVES 2 × 2 TIMES

A ingredients
2¼ cups (565 ml) water
1 tablespoon sake

5 oz (150 g) chicken tenders (remove any sinew)
Salt and freshly ground black pepper, to taste
1 bunch garlic chives (about 2 oz / 50 g)

B ingredients
1 teaspoon ground chili pepper
1 teaspoon soy sauce
½ teaspoon grated garlic
½ teaspoon grated ginger
1 teaspoon sesame oil
½ teaspoon white sesame seeds

1 Put the A ingredients in a pan over medium heat and bring to a boil. When it comes to a boil put in the chicken tenders and cook for 2 minutes. Put on a lid, turn off the heat and leave the pan for 5 minutes.
2 Take out the chicken tenders (reserve the cooking liquid) and cool until they can be handled. Shred into bite size pieces. Put the pieces into a bowl and add 2 tablespoons of the cooking liquid, salt and pepper and mix.
3 Cut the garlic chives into ¼-in (6-mm) long pieces. Blanch them briefly in the reserved cooking liquid, and drain into a colander. Add the garlic chives to the step-2 bowl, add the B ingredients, and mix to combine.

Quick and Easy Mixed Banchan

Mixed Semi-dried Fish and Bean Sprouts

 SHELF LIFE About 3 to 4 days in the refrigerator

Steaming makes the semi-dried horse mackerel plump and the bean sprouts flavorful. The crispy-crunchy texture of the bean sprouts is also pleasant.

SERVES 2 × 2 TIMES

1 aji no himono (semi-dried horse mackerel available at Asian markets)
1 tablespoon sake
2 cups bean sprouts (about 7 oz / 200 g)
2 or more teaspoons Seasoned Soy Sauce (➡ page 15)

> If using a microwave, cover each of the plates loosely with cling wrap. Cook the horse mackerel at 600 watts for 3 and a half minutes, and the bean sprouts for 3 minutes.

1 Put the semi-dried horse mackerel on a heatproof plate, and sprinkle with the sake. Set up a steamer* and heat until steam is rising from it. Set the plate with the fish on it in the steamer and steam cook over medium heat for 7 to 8 minutes. Leave until cool enough to handle, and remove the head and bones and shred the meat into bite-size pieces.

2 Remove the thin hairlike roots from the bean sprouts, and place the sprouts on a heatproof plate. Set in a steamer with steam rising from it and steam cook over medium heat for 5 minutes.

3 Put the step-1 and step-2 ingredients in a bowl. Add the Seasoned Soy Sauce and mix.

> * To set up a steamer, fill a large pot with water, place a steamer basket or other insert above the surface of the water, set in the item to be steamed, cover the pot, and bring the water to a boil.

Basic Banchan

Spicy Mixed Sashimi and Aromatic Vegetables

Chogochujang Sauce with added acidity gives sashimi a different taste! In addition to white fish, this sauce can also be used with squid sashimi or pickled mackerel.

 **SHELF LIFE** About 2 to 3 days in the refrigerator

SERVES 2 × 2 TIMES

- 5 oz (150 g) white fish sashimi (sea bream or similar fish)
- 2 cups loosely packed mitsuba (a refreshing green herb available at Asian markets) (about 1 oz / 30 g)
- 2 green onions (scallions)
- ⅙ onion
- Red and green chili peppers, to taste
- 3 tablespoons Chogochujang Sauce (➡ page 26)
- 1 teaspoon sesame oil

1 Slice the sashimi into thin diagonal slivers. Cut the mitsuba and green onions into 2-in (4- to 5-cm) long pieces, and thinly slice the onion. Slice the chili peppers into thin diagonal pieces.

2 Put the sliced sashimi in a bowl, add 1 tablespoon of Chogochujang Sauce and mix. Add the vegetables and the sesame oil, plus the remaining Chogochujang Sauce. Mix.

> If you sandwich the white fish sashimi between layers of dried kombu seaweed and leave to marinate for a few hours before using, it will be less watery.

Spicy Mixed Octopus and Spinach

 **SHELF LIFE** About 2 to 3 days in the refrigerator

SERVES 2 × 2 TIMES

4 oz (100 g) boiled octopus
5 cups loosely packed spinach (about 5 oz / 150 g)
½ teaspoon soy sauce
2 tablespoons Chogochujang Sauce (➡ see below)
Roasted white sesame seeds, to taste

1 Cut the boiled octopus up into bite-size pieces.
2 Blanch the spinach briefly in boiling water and drain into a colander. Cool under cold running water, and squeeze out well. Cut into 1¼-in (3-cm) pieces. Mix the spinach with the soy sauce.
3 Put the step-1 and step-2 ingredients in a bowl, add the Chogochujang Sauce and mix. Sprinkle on some sesame seeds.

> The umami of squid and Chogochujang Sauce go well together! Each diner can adjust the spiciness of the sauce to their liking by serving it separately.

Boiled Squid and Green Onions with Spicy Sauce

 **SHELF LIFE** About 2 to 3 days in the refrigerator

SERVES 2 × 2 TIMES

7 to 8 oz (200 to 250 g) fresh squid
⅓ Japanese leek or large green onion (scallion)

A ingredients
2½ cups (625 ml) water
1 tablespoon mirin
½ teaspoon salt

2 tablespoons Chogochujang Sauce (➡ see below)

1 Pull the arms off the squid, remove the guts and eyes, and peel off the skin. Cut the body up into circles, and the arms into bite-size pieces. Cut the Japanese leek or large green onion into 2-in (4- to 5-cm) long strips.

> Can be stored mixed with the sauce too.

2 Put the A ingredients in a pan over medium heat. When it comes to a boil add the step-1 ingredients and blanch briefly. Drain into a colander.
3 Put the step-2 ingredients on a serving plate and serve with the Chogochujang Sauce on the side.

NOTE

Chogochujang Sauce

This is a refreshing sauce made by adding vinegar (*sikcho*) to gochujang. It is one of the most popular sauces in South Korea, and is often abbreviated as "chojang." It goes well with fish and seafood, and is usually served with white fish or squid sashimi. It's also served with blanched wakame seaweed or bitter vegetables like bitter gourd. I also recommend using it for *bibimmyeon* (bibim noodles). You can also make it with freshly squeezed lemon juice instead of vinegar.

 SHELF LIFE About 2 to 3 days in the refrigerator

AN EASY-TO-MAKE AMOUNT

3 tablespoons gochujang
1 tablespoon rice vinegar
2 teaspoons sugar
1 teaspoon grated garlic

Combine all the ingredients and mix well.

26 Basic Banchan

Two ingredients with different textures are combined with a spicy flavor. A perfect dish to accompany the slight bitterness of beer.

Cucumber with Gochujang

 About 4 to 5 days in the refrigerator

SERVES 2 × 2 TIMES

2 baby cucumbers
½ teaspoon salt
½ teaspoon mulyeot (or honey)

A ingredients
2 tablespoons gochujang
1 teaspoon mulyeot (or honey)
1 teaspoon grated garlic
1 teaspoon roasted white sesame seeds

1 Peel 3 strips off the cucumbers using a vegetable peeler. Cut into scant ¼-in (5-mm) thick slices. Rub the salt and *mulyeot* (or honey) into the cucumber slices, and leave for 10 minutes.
2 Squeeze out the excess moisture from the cucumber slices, and mix with the A ingredients.

> If you store this dish in the refrigerator some moisture will come out of the cucumber, but you can eat it as is, or pour the whole dish with the exuded moisture over somen noodles.

Root Vegetables with Perilla

 About 4 to 5 days in the refrigerator

SERVES 2 × 2 TIMES

1 small carrot (about 2 oz / 50 g)
1 small Asian sweet potato (about 4 oz / 100 g)
1 lotus root (about 4 oz / 100 g)

A ingredients
3 tablespoons dried perilla powder
2 tablespoons Dried Anchovy Dashi Stock (➡ page 4)
⅓ teaspoon salt
⅓ teaspoon grated garlic

1 Wash all the root vegetables well without peeling them, and cut into small pieces. Bring water to a boil in a pan, and boil first the carrot, then the sweet potato and finally the lotus root, and drain into a colander.
2 Put the boiled vegetables into a bowl, add the A ingredients and mix.

> Three kinds of root vegetables are coated with perilla powder. The savory and unique flavor spreads in the mouth, and the texture is great too.

Spicy Daikon Radish

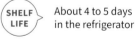 About 4 to 5 days in the refrigerator

SERVES 2 × 2 TIMES

½ small daikon radish (about 7 oz / 200 g)
½ teaspoon salt
1 teaspoon ground chili pepper

A ingredients
1 teaspoon fish sauce
1 teaspoon sugar
1 teaspoon rice vinegar
½ teaspoon grated garlic

1 Thinly slice the daikon radish, then cut the slices into thin matchsticks. Sprinkle with salt and leave for about 10 minutes. When the daikon radish is wilted, rinse the matchsticks briefly and squeeze out the excess moisture.
2 Put the daikon radish in a bowl, sprinkle evenly with the ground chili pepper, add the A ingredients and mix.

> The chili pepper powder add a spicy kick, and the fish sauce and garlic add depth to the dish.

Steamed Garlic Chives with Roasted Soybean Powder

About 3 to 4 days in the refrigerator

After adding the roasted soybean powder to the garlic chives, lift them up lightly with both hands several times to evenly coat the garlic chives with the powder.

SERVES 2 × 2 TIMES

- 2 bunches garlic chives (about 4 oz / 100 g)
- 1 tablespoon roasted soybean powder (*kangguru* in Korean, *kinako* in Japanese)
- 1 tablespoon Seasoned Soy Sauce (➡ page 15)

> In Korea, roasted soybean powder is an all-purpose coating. It subdues the odor of garlic chives.

1 Wash the garlic chives and drain. Cut into 2-in (4- to 5-cm) long pieces. Put into a heatproof container, coat with the roasted soybean flour and mix well.

2 Put the step-1 container into a steamer with the steam rising from it, and steam over medium heat for 5 minutes. (Alternatively, cover loosely with cling wrap and microwave at 600 watts for 2 minutes.)

3 Add the Seasoned Soy Sauce and mix well.

Basic Banchan

Mixed Eggplant and Myoga Ginger

SHELF LIFE: About 3 to 4 days in the refrigerator

SERVES 2 × 2 TIMES

2 small Asian eggplants
1 myoga ginger bud
Dash of salt
½ tablespoon Seasoned Soy Sauce (➡ page 15)
1 teaspoon perilla oil

1 Cut the tops off the eggplants, wrap each one in cling wrap and microwave one at a time at 600 watts for 2 minutes. Cut the myoga ginger buds into thin strips.
2 When the eggplants have cooled down enough to handle, cut them lengthwise into bite-size strips and place them into a bowl.
3 Add the myoga ginger, dash of salt, Seasoned Soy sauce and perilla oil to the eggplants and mix.

Myoga ginger is known for its edible mauve buds. You can substitute sliced shallots with a little minced fresh ginger for myoga ginger.

Eggplant can be easily heated in a microwave oven. The aroma of the myoga ginger is refreshing.

Mixed Broccoli and Shiitake Mushrooms

SHELF LIFE: About 3 to 4 days in the refrigerator

SERVES 2 × 2 TIMES

½ head broccoli (about 5 oz / 150 g)
3 raw shiitake mushrooms

A ingredients
1 tablespoon rice vinegar
1 tablespoon perilla oil
1 tablespoon ume syrup
⅓ teaspoon salt

1 Divide the broccoli into florets, boil briefly in hot water and drain into a colander.
2 Remove the hard stem ends from the shiitake mushrooms, and cut the stems off the caps. Cut the caps into 6 pieces each. Place on a heated grill upside down together with the stems, and grill until wilted. Shred the stems.
3 Put the step-1 and step-2 ingredients in a bowl. Add the combined A ingredients and mix well.

Broccoli infused with the umami flavor of shiitake mushrooms is delicious. The sour sauce makes it refreshing.

Eggplant can be easily heated in a microwave oven. The aroma of the myoga ginger is refreshing.

Nori Seaweed with Yangnyeom Sauce

Sliced Zucchini with Walnuts

Nori Seaweed with Yangnyeom Sauce

 About 1 week in the refrigerator

All you have to do is to add fragrant Yangnyeom Sauce to crispy nori seaweed. You won't be able to stop eating this on top of rice or noodles!

SERVES 2 × 2 TO 3 TIMES

5 full sheets nori seaweed (about 8 × 7 in / 21 × 19 cm each)
2 tablespoons sake or water

For the Yangnyeom Sauce
2 tablespoons Seasoned Soy Sauce (➡ page 15)
2 tablespoons finely minced green onion (scallion)
2 tablespoons coarsely minced onion
1 teaspoon roasted white sesame seeds
1 teaspoon sesame oil
½ teaspoon ground chili pepper, or to taste

1 Briefly crisp up the nori seaweed sheets in a dry hot skillet on both sides. Place the nori sheets in a plastic bag and knead the bag to crumble the nori finely. Transfer the nori to a bowl, add the sake or water and mix until the nori is softened.
2 Add the Yangnyeom Sauce ingredients and mix.

Sliced Zucchini with Walnuts

 About 3 to 4 days in the refrigerator

The freshness of raw zucchini goes well with the richness of the walnuts.
I use yellow zucchini, but green will also work.

SERVES 2 × 2 TIMES

1 small zucchini (about 5 oz / 150 g)
⅓ teaspoon salt
4–5 shelled walnuts (around 1 oz / 30 g)

A ingredients
1 tablespoon Dried Anchovy Dashi Stock (➡ page 4)
1 teaspoon soy sauce
1 teaspoon perilla oil
¼ teaspoon grated garlic

1 Slice the zucchini into thin rounds and sprinkle with the salt. Leave for about a minute, rinse and squeeze out excess moisture.
2 Chop the walnuts roughly.
3 Combine the step-1 and step-2 ingredients in a bowl, add the A ingredients and mix well.

Namul Vegetable Side Dishes

Made with seasonal vegetables, seaweed and mushrooms, namul are banchan that are an indispensable part of the Korean diet. Here are four different seasonings to match the colors and flavors of the ingredients.

- Eggplant and Eggplant Skin Namul
- Bean Sprout Namul
- Okra Namul
- Carrot Namul

Simple Namuls

SHELF LIFE — About 2 to 3 days in the refrigerator

This is a good way to bring out the gentle colors of vegetables, such as white and orange. In general, vegetables should be lightly boiled and steamed before mixing with the Salt-based Namul Seasoning, but carrots should be stir-fried in oil to enhance their umami flavor.

AN EASY-TO-MAKE AMOUNT

For the Salt-based Namul Seasoning
- ¼ teaspoon salt
- ¼ teaspoon grated garlic
- 1 teaspoon perilla oil (or sesame oil)

Eggplant and Eggplant Skin Namul

Peel the eggplants for a slippery texture.

1 Take the tops off 2 small Asian eggplants, and peel off the skin with a vegetable peeler (reserve the skins).
2 Wrap each peeled eggplant in cling wrap, and microwave each one individually for 2 minutes at 600 watts. When they are cool enough to handle, tear lengthwise into bite-size pieces.
3 Add the Salt-based Namul Seasoning and add ½ tablespoon perilla powder. Mix well.

> **Turn the eggplant skins into namul too!**
> Slice the eggplant skins into thin strips diagonally. Soak in water, changing the water 2 to 3 times to get rid of the bitterness. Drain well, squeeze out any excess moisture, and mix with a little salt and perilla oil.

Bean Sprout Namul

A namul staple with a pleasant crunchy texture.

1 Remove the thin hairlike roots from 2 cups (about 7 oz / 200 g) of bean sprouts, and boil the sprouts for 3 minutes. Drain into a colander.
2 Add the Salt-based Namul Seasoning and mix.

Okra Namul

Cut into thin lengthwise strips, and mix well with the seasoning.

1 Boil 10 okra pods briefly, cool with cold water, and drain into a colander.
2 Cut off the stems diagonally, and cut each pod into 6 strips. Add the Salt-based Namul Seasoning and mix well. Sprinkle with a little perilla powder.

Carrot Namul

Stir-fry in oil to give the carrot a rich flavor and lock in the umami.

1 Peel 1 carrot, slice it diagonally, and cut it into thin matchsticks.
2 Heat up 1 teaspoon of rapeseed or canola oil in a skillet over medium heat. Add the step-1 carrot and sprinkle with ¼ teaspoon salt. Stir-fry slowly.
3 Add ¼ teaspoon grated garlic and 1 teaspoon sesame oil and mix.

NOTE

Besides the vegetables described here, daikon radish, turnip, cucumber, asparagus, lotus root and bamboo shoot go well with the Salt-based Namul Seasoning.

Soy Sauce Namuls

Soy Sauce Namuls

SHELF LIFE — About 2 to 3 days in the refrigerator

The aroma and umami of soy sauce is delicious with these ingredients and goes well with garlic too. It is good with dark green vegetables, flavorful seaweeds, and umami-rich mushrooms.

AN EASY-TO-MAKE AMOUNT

For the Soy Sauce Namul Seasoning
- 1 teaspoon soy sauce
- ⅓ teaspoon grated garlic
- 1 teaspoon perilla oil (or sesame oil)

Garlic Chive Namul

Garlic chives and garlic double the aroma and whet your appetite.

1 Blanch 2 bunches of garlic chives briefly. Cool in cold water, and squeeze out the excess moisture. Cut into 1½-in (4-cm) long pieces.
2 Add the Soy Sauce Namul Seasoning and mix.

Wakame Seaweed Namul

Use thick salt-preserved wakame seaweed for this. Sprinkle with sesame seeds for a nutty flavor.

1 Soak 1 cup of salt-cured wakame seaweed in water, and rinse off the salt well. Cut into bite-size pieces, and drain off any excess moisture.
2 Add the Soy Sauce Namul Seasoning and mix. Sprinkle with some roasted white sesame seeds.

Mushroom Namul

The green onions add a nice flavor accent to the umami of the mushrooms.

1 Pull apart 2 cups of maitake mushrooms into small clumps (or use any fresh mushroom of your choice) and blanch briefly in boiling water. Drain into a colander. (Alternatively, microwave the mushrooms for 2 minutes.)
2 Add the Soy Sauce Namul Seasoning and mix. Sprinkle with a little minced green onion (scallion).

Saltwort Namul

This vegetable has a unique crunchy texture and a refreshing aroma.

1 Cook 2 cups of saltwort or spinach for 1 minute in boiling water. Drain into a colander. Cut into bite-size pieces.
2 Combine with the Soy Sauce Namul Seasoning and mix.

> **Saltwort** has slender, bright green, succulent-like stems that taste mildly salty and are slightly crunchy. You can substitute blanched spinach or young asparagus tips for saltwort.

NOTE

Besides the vegetables above, finely cut kombu seaweed, dried shiitake mushrooms, mountain herbs such as bracken and ostrich (fiddlehead) fern work well with the Soy Sauced Namul Seasoning. If you want to make an eggplant namul without peeling them, I recommend using this seasoning mix.

Soy Sauce and Doenjang Namuls

Soy Sauce and Doenjang Namuls

 **SHELF LIFE** About 4 days in the refrigerator

Adding *doenjang* (Korean miso) to soy sauce gives it a rich and unique taste. I like to use this seasoning for leafy vegetable namuls.

AN EASY-TO-MAKE AMOUNT

For the Soy Sauce and Doenjang Namul Seasoning
½ teaspoon soy sauce
1 teaspoon doenjang (or Japanese miso)
⅓ teaspoon grated garlic
1 teaspoon perilla oil (or sesame oil)

> **Doenjang** is a traditional Korean fermented soybean paste. It is thick, brown and chunky, with a savory, salty and slightly earthy flavor. You can substitute Japanese miso paste for *doenjang*.

Bitter Gourd Namul

The bitterness is mellowed by the doenjang.

1 Cut half of a bitter gourd in half lengthwise and remove the seeds and pith. Slice thinly. Sprinkle with a pinch of salt and leave for a while. Rinse well, and squeeze out the excess moisture.
2 Add the Soy Sauce and Doenjang Namul Seasoning and mix well.

Broccoli Namul

Boil the broccoli for a short time to preserve its crunchy texture.

1 Divide half a head of a broccoli into florets (about 1 cup). Cook for 1 minute in boiling water, and drain into a colander.
2 Add the Soy Sauce and Doenjang Namul Seasoning and mix well.

Water Celery Namul

The unique aroma of water celery blends well with the soy sauce and doenjang.

1 Blanch 1 bunch of water celery, cool in cold water and squeeze out the excess moisture. Cut into 1½-in (3- to 4-cm) long pieces.
2 Add the Soy Sauce and Doenjang Namul Seasoning and mix well. Sprinkle with a little perilla powder.

> **Water celery** has a fresh, peppery flavor. You can substitute Italian parsley or young celery leaves for water celery.

Komatsuna Greens Namul

The doenjang increases the umami of the vegetables.

1 Blanch 1 bunch of *komatsuna* greens, cool in cold water and squeeze out the excess moisture. Cut into 1½-in (3- to 4-cm) long pieces.
2 Add the Soy Sauce and Doenjang Namul Seasoning and mix well. Sprinkle with some roasted white sesame seeds.

> **Komatsuna** is mild and slightly peppery-sweet. You can substitute spinach, bok choy or Swiss chard for *komatsuna*.

NOTE

Besides the vegetables above, napa cabbage, chrysanthemum greens, shirona cabbage, bok choy, mizuna greens, broccolini or other leafy greens can be used with this seasoning. It is also recommended for when you want to increase the umami and richness of root vegetables such as burdock root and lotus root.

Gochujang Namuls

Hijiki Seaweed Namul

Wood Ear Mushroom Namul

Japanese Leek Namul

Aralia Erata Shoot Namul

Gochujang Namuls

 About 4 to 5 days in the refrigerator

Namuls based on sweet and spicy gochujang. It goes well with ingredients with unique flavors, so it is perfect for when you want a change of pace from the usual namul.

AN EASY-TO-MAKE AMOUNT

For the Gochujang Namul Seasoning
1 tablespoon gochujang
½ teaspoon soy sauce
⅓ teaspoon grated garlic
⅓ teaspoon ground chili pepper

NOTE

The Gochujang Namul Seasoning goes well with wild mountain herbs such as ostrich (fiddlehead) fern and hosta, as well as slightly spicy vegetables such as long-stamen chives and leafy garlic. For a refreshing taste, use Chogochujang Sauce with vinegar (➡ page 26) as a base.

Hijiki Seaweed Namul

Use hijiki seaweed with good flavor and texture.

1 Soak 1 cup of dried hijiki seaweed in water until it is rehydrated. Pour boiling water over the hijiki seaweed and drain into a colander.
2 Add the Gochujang Namul Seasoning and mix. Sprinkle with some roasted white sesame seeds.

Wood Ear Mushroom Namul

The crunchy texture makes this an excellent snack or side dish.

1 Soak ½ cup of dried wood ear mushrooms in water until rehydrated. Cut off the tough stem ends, Boil briefly in hot water and drain into a colander. Cut into bite-size pieces.
2 Add the Gochujang Namul Seasoning and mix.

Japanese Leek Namul

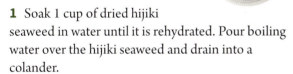

Use the white parts, which becomes sweeter when boiled.

1 Slice the white part of 1 Japanese leek or large green onion (scallion) into 2-in (4- to 5-cm) long strips. Blanch briefly in boiling water and drain into a colander. Pat dry with paper towels.
2 Add the Gochujang Namul Seasoning and mix. Sprinkle with some roasted white sesame seeds.

Aralia Erata Shoot Namul

A mature taste with a hint of bitterness from the aralia erata shoot.

1 Cook 2½ cups of *aralia erata* shoots (Japanese angelica tree shoots) for 1 minute in boiling water, and drain into a colander. Cool in cold water, and squeeze out the excess moisture.
2 Add the Gochujang Namul Seasoning and mix. Sprinkle on a little rice vinegar to taste.

Aralia elata shoots have a slightly bitter, nutty and earthy flavor. You can substitute fiddlehead ferns or asparagus for *aralia elata* shoots.

Kimchis

Kimchi, the best known Korean pickled vegetables, are a staple of banchan. While authentic pickled kimchi requires a lot of time and effort, instant kimchi that is simply mixed with a sauce can be prepared anytime. Quick pickled kimchi, which does not use chili peppers, and water kimchi, which allows you to savor the juices, are perfect for change-of-pace dishes.

Instant Napa Cabbage Kimchi

About 3 weeks in the refrigerator

This instant kimchi has a spicy yet sweet and refreshing taste. You can regard it like a salad and eat as much as you like.

AN EASY-TO-MAKE AMOUNT

- ½ medium napa or Chinese cabbage (about 1 lb / 500 g)
- One 1¼-in (3-cm) piece daikon radish
- 1 tablespoon coarse salt
- ⅓ Japanese leek or large green onion (scallion)
- 3 to 4 tablespoon Kimchi Sauce (➜ see below)

1 Peel off each leaf of the napa cabbage, cut them into half lengthwise and then slice into diagonal pieces (a). Slice the daikon radish into thin rounds, then shred finely. Combine both vegetables in a bowl, sprinkle with salt and leave for a while.

2 When the vegetables have exuded moisture and the napa cabbage stems are wilted, rinse off the salt briefly, drain into a colander, and leave to drain (b).

3 Slice the leek or green onion in half lengthwise, then thinly slice on the diagonal.

4 Combine the vegetables from steps 2 and 3 in a bowl, add the Kimchi Sauce and mix well (c).

> To prevent exposure to air, put the kimchi in a food storage bag with the air pressed out. If using a storage container, cover the surface of the kimchi tightly with cling wrap. Do not change storage containers during storage. When the kimchi turns sour, use it in stir-fries or stews.

a

Peel each napa cabbage leaf one by one and cut with a knife along the fibers from top to bottom, then cut diagonally.

b

Leave the salted napa cabbage and daikon radish in a colander for a while to drain off naturally. The key is to not squeeze it out.

c

Add the Kimchi Sauce and mix evenly and thoroughly with your hands to let the flavors permeate the vegetables.

NOTE

Kimchi Sauce

SHELF LIFE About 2 to 3 weeks in the refrigerator

This sauce has ingredients such as *saeujeot* and fish sauce that become the source of umami in kimchi made with it. Let it mature for half a day in the summer, and a whole day in other seasons before storing it in the refrigerator. In 2 to 3 days the sauce will mature and become well rounded in flavor!

AN EASY-TO-MAKE AMOUNT

- 1 tablespoon saeujeot (fermented mysid shrimp preserved in salt)
- 3 tablespoons ground chili pepper
- 2 tablespoons grated Asian pear or apple
- 2 tablespoons grated onion
- 1 tablespoon grated garlic
- ½ tablespoon grated ginger
- 1 tablespoon fish sauce
- 1 tablespoon ume syrup
- 1 teaspoon sugar

1 Finely mince the *saeujeot* (you can also chop it up in a food processor). Combine it with the other ingredients. Mix well.

2 Put into a storage container and leave at room temperature for half a day to a whole day. Transfer to the refrigerator.

Three Kinds of Instant Kimchi

SHELF LIFE — About 1 week in the refrigerator

Use the Kimchi Sauce (➡ page 43) to make instant kimchi with other vegetables.

Cherry Tomato Kimchi

The spiciness of the sauce blends with the acidity and sweetness of the tomatoes, resulting in a succulent taste.

1 Remove the tops from 20 cherry tomatoes and make shallow crisscross cuts in each tomato. Blanch briefly in boiling water and peel the tomatoes. Thinly slice ¼ of an onion.
2 Put the step-1 ingredients in a bowl, add 2 to 3 tablespoons of the Kimchi Sauce and mix well.

Daikon Radish Kimchi

Fresh raw daikon radishes are crisp and refreshing. Use the slightly bitter leaves too.

1 Cut 3 small daikon radishes with their leaves on (about 12 oz / 350 g) into wedges without peeling them. Cut the leaves into 1¼-in (3-cm) long pieces.
2 Put the step-1 daikon radishes and greens into a bowl, sprinkle with ½ teaspoon salt and leave for a while. When the leaves are wilted, rinse briefly and drain into a colander.
3 Mix well with 2 to 3 tablespoons of the Kimchi Sauce.

Bashed Cucumber Kimchi

Bash the cucumber to allow the flavors to permeate it. Combine with garlic chives for a nice aroma.

1 Sprinkle 3 baby cucumbers with a little salt and roll them back and forth firmly on a cutting board. Bash them lightly with a rolling pin or a pestle to break them. Cut them into 1½- to 2-in (4- to 5-cm) long pieces.
2 Put the cucumber pieces in a bowl, sprinkle with ½ teaspoon salt and leave for a while. Rinse briefly and drain into a colander.
3 Return the cucumber to a bowl, add 2 tablespoons of the Kimchi Sauce and mix well.

Cherry Tomato Kimchi — Bashed Cucumber Kimchi — Daikon Radish Kimchi

Chopped Napa Cabbage Kimchi with Yuzu

 SHELF LIFE About 1 week in the refrigerator

This kimchi without chili peppers is popular among students in my cooking classes. It requires a little work to prepare the ingredients, but once that is done all you need to do is mix them together to create a rich, deeply flavored kimchi.

AN EASY-TO-MAKE AMOUNT

¼ napa cabbage (about 1 lb / 500 g)
1 tablespoon salt

A ingredients

Zest from ¼ ripe yuzu fruit
¼ Asian pear, sliced
2 dried jujubes, sliced
1 tablespoon pine nuts
2 raw chestnuts, peeled and thinly sliced
1 clove garlic, sliced
One 1-in (2.5-cm) piece fresh ginger, peeled and sliced
2 green onions (scallions) (about 1 oz / 30 g), cut into 1½-in (4-cm) long pieces
3 stalks water celery, cut into 1½-in (4-cm) long pieces
1 tablespoon saeujeot (fermented mysid shrimp preserved in salt)

1 Peel off each leaf of the napa cabbage, cut them into half lengthwise and then slice into diagonal pieces. Place the napa cabbage in a bowl and sprinkle with the salt, and leave for a while. When the napa cabbage is wilted, rinse off briefly, drain into a colander and leave to drain naturally.
2 Mix the A ingredients together, add the step-1 napa cabbage and mix to combine.
3 Put into a storage container and leave to ferment for half a day to a full day at room temperature. Transfer the storage container to the refrigerator.

Kimchis 45

A non-spicy kimchi with the gentle sweetness of Asian pear. It is a perfect little side dish that can be stored in the refrigerator and enjoyed for a long time.

Rolled Napa Cabbage Kimchi

 2 to 3 months in the refrigerator

AN EASY-TO-MAKE AMOUNT

10 small leaves napa cabbage (about 1 lb, 10 oz / 800 g)
1 tablespoon salt

Pickling Liquid ingredients

1 tablespoon salt
1 teaspoon sugar
¾ cup, plus 1 tablespoon (200 ml) water

A ingredients

1 cup thinly sliced daikon radish (about 5 oz / 150 g)
¼ Asian pear, sliced
2 cloves garlic, sliced
1 piece fresh ginger, peeled and thinly sliced
⅔ teaspoon salt
A pinch of dried chili pepper threads, if available

Cut into bite-size pieces before eating.

1 Sprinkle each of the napa cabbage leaves with salt, concentrating on the stem parts. Layer the leaves in a shallow tray or container, sprinkle with a little water, place a weight on them (a 2-liter water bottle for example) and leave for about half a day.

2 When the stems of the napa cabbage leaves are wilted enough to bend them easily without

If the stem end parts of the napa cabbage leaves are too thick, slice them off, thinly slice the shaved off part and wrap in the leaves together with the A ingredients.

breaking, rinse the leaves and drain into a colander. Leave to dry naturally.

3 Combine the Pickling Liquid ingredients in a pan and bring to a boil. Turn off the heat and leave to cool.

4 Combine the A ingredients in a bowl.

5 Spread out each of the step-2 napa cabbage leaves, place some of the combined A ingredients on the stem end of each. Roll up each leaf (photo at left).

6 Place each of the rolled napa cabbage leaves in a storage container with the loose ends underneath. Pour the step-3 Pickling Liquid over them. Leave at room temperature for half a day to a full day, then transfer to the refrigerator.

Water Kimchi with Citrus

SHELF LIFE: 1 to 2 months in the refrigerator

AN EASY-TO-MAKE AMOUNT

2 to 3 leaves napa cabbage (4 oz / 100 g)
1 small daikon radish (about 5 oz / 150 g)
½ tablespoon coarse salt
½ tablespoon sugar
1 cup citrus fruit segments (about 2 fruits, or 8 oz / 250 g) of your choice (such as mandarin orange, clementine, Chinese honey orange, iyokan orange, amanatsu orange, etc.)

A ingredients

2 cloves garlic, thinly sliced
½ teaspoon ginger juice
Red chili pepper, thinly sliced, to taste
2 cups (500 ml) bottled mineral water
½ tablespoon salt
½ teaspoon sugar

1 Cut the napa cabbage and daikon radish into ¾-in (2-cm) squares, sprinkle with the coarse salt and sugar and leave for about 30 minutes.
2 Remove the peels and membranes from the citrus fruit, and pull the fruit apart into small pieces (if using mandarin oranges, you do not have to subdivide the sections.)
3 Combine the A ingredients in a storage container and add the step-1 and step-2 ingredients, juices and all.
4 Leave the storage container at room temperature for half a day to a full day. Transfer to the refrigerator and leave to mature for at least 5 days (if possible, leave for about 2 weeks to maximize the umami).

Add a little water celery and / or shredded red chili pepper as garnish when serving.

This is a cool water kimchi served with the juice. The citrus flavor is refreshing. The longer it is left in the sun, the more it ferments and the more umami it will have.

Dongchimi or daikon radish water kimchi promotes digestion and goes well with meat dishes. The acidic pickling juice (from lactic acid producing bacteria) is also a treat and can be used as a soup for cold noodles.

Daikon Radish Water Kimchi

SHELF LIFE: 1 to 2 months in the refrigerator

AN EASY-TO-MAKE AMOUNT

½ small daikon radish (about 7 oz / 200 g)
4 green onions (scallions)
1 red chili pepper
1 green chili pepper
1 tablespoon coarse salt

A ingredients

4 cups (1 liter) mineral water
1½ tablespoons coarse salt
1 tablespoon sugar
½ Korean pear (or 1 Asian pear), cut into wedges with its skin on (about 7 to 8 oz / 200 to 250 g)
4 cloves garlic, thinly sliced
One 2-in (5 cm)-piece fresh ginger, peeled and thinly sliced

To serve, cut the daikon radish into bite-size pieces and put them into a bowl with the chili peppers and the green onions.

1 Cut the unpeeled daikon radish into quarters lengthwise (a). Put into a bowl with the green onions and chili peppers and sprinkle with the coarse salt. Leave at room temperature for half a day to a full day.

2 Fold up the green onions from step 1 into 2-in (5-cm) long bundles, wrap the ends around the bundle and secure.

3 Combine the A ingredients in a plastic zip-top bag, and add the drained daikon radish, chili pepper and step-2 green onions (b).

4 Leave the storage container at room temperature for half a day to a full day. Transfer to the refrigerator and leave to mature for at least 5 days (if possible, leave for about 2 weeks to maximize the umami).

a

Cut the daikon radish into large pieces before pickling. I recommend trying this with sweet winter daikon radish!

b

Put the vegetables in a zipped food storage bag to pickle. Try not to open the bag while the pickling process is ongoing.

Basic Banchan

PART 2
Side Dishes and Main Dishes

Whether it is a hearty stir-fry, a tasty simmered dish that can be made in quantity for extra flavor, or a jeon made with seasonal vegetables, banchan are not only side dishes, but also main dishes and snacks to serve with drinks. They can be enjoyed not only eaten as-is, but also wrapped in leafy greens or served over rice.

Stir-fries

Stir-fries make great banchan to have as a side dish as well as a main dish. The key is to season the ingredients before stir-frying.

Beef Bulgogi

SHELF LIFE: 3 to 4 days in the refrigerator

The secret to great taste is to let the meat and vegetables marinate in the sauce for a while to allow the flavors to blend well. Mushrooms, such as enoki mushrooms and king oyster mushrooms, also work well in this dish.

SERVES 2 × 2 TIMES

- 7 oz (200 g) beef shoulder, very thinly sliced
- 3 tablespoons grated Asian pear (or apple)
- ½ onion
- ½ Japanese leek or large green onion (scallion)
- ⅓ red chili pepper
- ⅓ green chili pepper
- 4 tablespoons Bulgogi Sauce (➡ see below)
- 1 teaspoon rapeseed or canola oil

1 Cut the beef into 2-in (5-cm) pieces and place into a bowl. Add the grated Asian pear (or apple) and mix. Leave for 15 minutes.

2 Thinly slice the onion, and cut the leek or green onion and chili peppers into thin diagonal pieces.

3 Add the step-2 ingredients and the Bulgogi Sauce to the step-1 bowl and mix well. Refrigerate for at least 30 minutes to let the flavors permeate the beef (photo at right).

4 Heat up the oil in a skillet over medium heat, add the step-3 ingredients and stir-fry until cooked through.

The beef mixture can be stored while it is marinating. It will keep in the refrigerator for 2 to 3 days this way. If you let it marinate overnight or longer, it will be tastier and the beef will be more tender.

NOTE

Bulgogi Sauce

This flavorful stir-fry sauce has a fruity sweetness from the addition of grated Asian pear. It is versatile enough for stir-frying beef, chicken, pork, squid, scallops and so on.

SHELF LIFE: About 2 weeks in the refrigerator

AN EASY-TO-MAKE AMOUNT

- 3 tablespoons soy sauce
- 3 tablespoons grated onion
- 3 tablespoons grated Asian pear (or apple)
- 1 tablespoon ume syrup
- ½ tablespoon sugar
- ½ tablespoon grated garlic
- 1 teaspoon roasted white sesame seeds
- 1 teaspoon sesame oil
- Pinch of freshly ground black pepper

Combine all the ingredients and mix well.

Stir-fries 51

Pork Belly with Gochujang

A Korean-style stir-fry with spicy-sweet Gochujang Sauce. Wrap it with leafy greens such as perilla leaves or salad greens. Serving it with fresh green chili peppers, which you can nibble from time to time, is the Korean way.

SERVES 2 × 2 TIMES

7 oz (200 g) pork belly, very thinly sliced
½ onion
½ Japanese leek or large green onion (scallion)
4 tablespoons Gochujang Sauce (➡ see below)
1 teaspoon rapeseed or canola oil
1 teaspoon roasted white sesame seeds

1 Cut the pork belly into 2-in (4- to 5-cm) wide pieces. Thinly slice the onion, and cut the leek or green onion into thin diagonal pieces.
2 Put the step-1 ingredients in a bowl, add the Gochujang Sauce and mix.
3 Heat up the oil in a skillet over medium heat. Add the step-2 ingredients and stir-fry until the pork is cooked, and sprinkle with sesame seeds.

NOTE

Gochujang Sauce

This is a standard stir-fry sauce in South Korea. It is spicy yet sweet and rich at the same time, and can be used for meat or vegetable stir-fries.

AN EASY-TO-MAKE AMOUNT

3 tablespoons gochujang
½ tablespoon soy sauce
½ tablespoon ume syrup
½ teaspoon grated garlic
1 teaspoon ground red chili pepper
1 teaspoon sesame oil
Pinch of freshly ground black pepper

Combine all the ingredients and mix well.

Side Dishes and Main Dishes

Stir-fried Beef with Shishito Peppers and Garlic

Use your favorite cut of beef or offcuts. After the *mulyeot* has been rubbed into the beef, combine with plenty of garlic.

 SHELF LIFE — 3 to 4 days in the refrigerator

SERVES 2 × 2 TIMES

- 7 oz (200 g) beef, very thinly sliced
- 1 teaspoon mulyeot (or honey)
- 10 to 12 shishito peppers
- 3 cloves garlic, thinly sliced
- ½ tablespoon rapeseed or canola oil

A ingredients
- ¼ teaspoon salt
- Freshly ground black pepper, to taste
- 1 tablespoon sake
- 2 teaspoons soy sauce

1 Cut the beef into 1½-in (3- to 4-cm) wide pieces. Rub in the *mulyeot* (or honey). Open a hole in each shishito pepper with your fingernail.

2 Heat up the garlic and oil in a skillet over medium heat. When it is fragrant add the step-1 beef and stir-fry quickly. Add the A ingredients in the order listed and mix, then take the beef out of the skillet.

3 Quickly stir-fry the shishito peppers in the same skillet, and arrange on a serving plate with the step-2 beef.

Pork and Kimchi Stir-fry

SHELF LIFE: 3 to 4 days in the refrigerator

I recommend using kimchi that has turned sour through continuing fermentation. Stir-frying it well gives it a rich flavor, and the juices will thicken and coat the meat.

SERVES 2 × 2 TIMES

7 oz (200 g) pork, thinly cut and roughly chopped

A ingredients
- 1 tablespoon sake
- ½ tablespoon soy sauce
- 1 teaspoon grated garlic
- 1 teaspoon mulyeot (or honey)
- 1 teaspoon sesame oil

1⅓ cups napa cabbage kimchi
1 teaspoon rapeseed or canola oil
1 teaspoon roasted white sesame seeds
1 teaspoon sesame oil

1 Put the pork and the A ingredients in a bowl and mix. Roughly chop up the napa cabbage kimchi.
2 Heat up the rapeseed or canola oil in a skillet over medium heat, and stir-fry the pork. When the meat changes color, add the kimchi, and stir-fry slowly over medium-low heat for 7 to 8 minutes.
3 Sprinkle with the sesame seeds and drizzle on the sesame oil.

NOTE

Use the leftover cooking juices to make fried rice!

After making a stir-fry, making fried rice with the juices left in the skillet is something I look forward to. Press down the rice with a spatula to make Korean-style crispy rice. Try it with Beef Bulgogi or Pork Belly with Gochujang too!

Sweet and Spicy Chicken with Gochujang

 SHELF LIFE 3 to 4 days in the refrigerator

Simply pour Gochujang Sauce over the chicken and stir-fry. The addition of *mulyeot* at the end enhances the rich flavor.

SERVES 2 × 2 TIMES

- 7 oz (200 g) boneless chicken meat (dark or white meat)
- 4 tablespoons Gochujang Sauce (➡ page 52)
- 1 teaspoon rapeseed or canola oil
- 1 teaspoon mulyeot (or honey)

1 Cut the chicken into thin diagonal slivers, and rub in the Gochujang Sauce.

2 Heat up the oil in a skillet over medium heat, and stir-fry the step-1 chicken. When the chicken is cooked through, drizzle in the *mulyeot* (or honey) and turn off the heat.

> Serve this with plenty of shredded raw cabbage to make a refreshing dish.

Aromatic Stir-fried Chicken Gizzards

 SHELF LIFE 4 to 5 days in the refrigerator

The crunchy texture of the gizzards is irresistible. Add plenty of garlic chives and enjoy the aroma!

SERVES 2 × 2 TIMES

5 oz (150 g) chicken gizzards
¼ onion
⅓ Japanese leek or large green onion (scallion)
4 to 5 garlic chives
1 teaspoon rapeseed or canola oil
Salt and freshly ground black pepper, to taste
2 tablespoons Gochujang Sauce (➡ page 52)
1 tablespoon sake
1 teaspoon roasted white sesame seeds
1 teaspoon sesame oil

1 Wash the chicken gizzards and pat try. Remove the tough white sinew, make 2 to 3 cuts into each gizzard, and cut into bite-size pieces.
2 Thinly slice the onion, and mince the leek or green onion. Cut the garlic chives into 1¼-in (3-cm) long pieces.
3 Heat up the rapeseed or canola oil in a skillet over medium heat, and stir-fry the step-1 chicken gizzards. When they are cooked through add the salt and pepper, and put in the onion, leek or green onion, Gochujang Sauce and sake. Stir-fry together.
4 Add the garlic chives, sesame seeds and sesame oil and mix quickly. Turn off the heat.

Stir-fries   57

Asparagus and Onion Summer Japchae

SHELF LIFE: 3 to 4 days in the refrigerator

This early summer japchae has a refreshing green color.

SERVES 2 × 2 TIMES

- 4 stalks asparagus
- ½ onion
- 1 teaspoon, plus 1 tablespoon rapeseed or canola oil, divided
- Salt and freshly ground black pepper, to taste, divided
- 1 recipe prepared Korean Glass Noodles (➡ see below)
- Coarsely ground black pepper, for sprinkling

1 Boil the asparagus stalks briefly and cool in cold water. Drain and cut into thin diagonal slices. Thinly slice the onion.

2 Heat up 1 teaspoon of rapeseed or canola oil in a skillet over medium heat, and stir-fry the asparagus. When they are coated with oil, add a pinch each of salt and pepper, and transfer to a bowl.

3 Add the remaining tablespoon of rapeseed or canola oil to the skillet and stir-fry the onion. When it is wilted, add another pinch each of salt and pepper, and combine with the step-2 asparagus.

4 Add the prepared Korean glass noodles to the bowl and mix, and sprinkle with coarsely ground black pepper.

NOTE

Two Kinds of Japchae

Japchae (glass noodle dishes) have the reputation of being sweet and spicy, but here they are made with a salt-based seasoning, taking advantage of the beautiful colors of each season's ingredients.

Preparing Korean Glass Noodles

Korean glass noodles, called *dangmyeon* or "old fashioned glass noodles," are made of 100% sweet potato starch. They are thicker than Japanese glass noodles and are quite chewy. They have a springy texture and do not become limp even after some time, so they are perfect for make-ahead dishes like banchan.

Mushroom Autumn Japchae

This fall japchae is simply colored with the chic colors of mushrooms.

SHELF LIFE 3 to 4 days in the refrigerator

SERVES 2 × 2 TIMES

½ onion
1½ cups combined maitake and king oyster mushrooms (7 oz / 200 g)
1 teaspoon, plus 1 tablespoon rapeseed or canola oil, divided
Salt and freshly ground black pepper, to taste, divided
½ clove garlic, grated
1 recipe prepared Korean Glass Noodles (➡ see below)
Coarsely ground black pepper, for sprinkling

1 Thinly slice the onion. Separate the maitake mushrooms into small clumps, and cut the king oyster mushrooms into bite-size pieces.
2 Heat up 1 teaspoon of the rapeseed or canola oil in a skillet over medium heat, and stir-fry the onion. When it is wilted, sprinkle with a pinch each of salt and pepper, and transfer to a bowl.
3 Add the remaining tablespoon of rapeseed or canola oil and the garlic to the skillet over medium heat and quickly stir-fry the mushrooms. Add another pinch each of salt and pepper, and combine with the step-2 onion.
4 Add the prepared Korean glass noodles to the bowl and mix, and sprinkle with coarsely ground black pepper.

SERVES 2 × 2 TIMES

4 oz (100 g) dried dangmyeon (Korean glass noodles)

A ingredients
⅓ cup, plus 4 teaspoons (100 ml) Dried Anchovy Dashi Stock (➡ page 4)
2 teaspoons fish sauce
2 teaspoons sesame oil
1 teaspoon light soy sauce
⅔ teaspoon grated garlic

1 Bring a pot of water to a boil, cook the glass noodles for about 6 minutes, and drain into a colander.
2 Put all the A ingredients in a skillet over medium heat and bring to a boil. Add the step-1 glass noodles and cook until there is almost no moisture left in the pan.

Stir-fries 59

Kombu Seaweed with Garlic and Soy

 3 to 4 days in the refrigerator

Delicious *kiri-kombu* (cut-up, lightly seasoned kombu seaweed) with the aroma of garlic, dashi and soy sauce. Great as an accompaniment to alcoholic drinks.

SERVES 2 × 2 TIMES

1 teaspoon rapeseed or canola oil
2 cloves garlic, thinly sliced
2 cups kiri-kombu (about 5 oz / 150 g)
½ onion, thinly sliced
¼ small carrot, shredded

A ingredients

⅓ cup, plus 4 teaspoons (100 ml) Dried Anchovy Dashi Stock (➡ page 4)
2 teaspoons soy sauce
A pinch salt

1 teaspoon roasted white sesame seeds
½ teaspoon sesame oil

1 Heat up the rapeseed or canola oil in a skillet over medium heat, and stir-fry the garlic. When the garlic is fragrant, add the *kiri-kombu*, onion and carrot and stir-fry. Add the combined A ingredients and simmer.
2 When the liquid in the skillet has been reduced by half, add the sesame seeds and sesame oil and continue stir-frying until there is almost no liquid left in the skillet. Remove from the heat.

> **Kiri-kombu** is thinly shredded kelp. It appears as pale, ribbon-like strips and has a savory, umami-rich and slightly briny flavor. You can substitute finely sliced dashi kombu or wakame for *kiri-kombu*.

Sweet and Spicy Sakura Shrimp with Garlic Shoots

 5 to 6 days in the refrigerator

The savory taste of dried sakura shrimp is combined with the punchy flavor of garlic. This dish will stimulate your appetite!

SERVES 2 × 2 TIMES

¼ cup dried sakura shrimp (about ¾ oz / 20 g)
½ cup garlic shoots (about 3 oz / 80 g)

A ingredients

½ tablespoon mirin
½ tablespoon soy sauce
½ tablespoon sugar
1 teaspoon gochujang
1 teaspoon mulyeot (or honey)

Roasted white sesame seeds, for sprinkling

1 Dry-roast the sakura shrimp in an unoiled skillet. Empty out into a fine-meshed colander and shake off the fine dust.
2 Cut the garlic shoots into 2-in (4- to 5-cm) long pieces. Blanch briefly in boiling water.
3 Wipe out the skillet, add the combined A ingredients and bring to a boil. Add the step-1 sakura shrimp and mix. Add the step-2 garlic shoots and stir-fry. Sprinkle with sesame seeds.

> **Sakura shrimp** are tiny, pinkish-red shrimp native to Japan. In dried form, they have a sweet, briny and intensely umami flavor. You can substitute dried baby shrimp or finely chopped dried shrimp for sakura shrimp.

Stir-fries

Eggplant and Onion with Fragrant Miso

SHELF LIFE: 4 to 5 days in the refrigerator

A rich miso paste is used to season the lightly flavored eggplant. Either Korean *doenjang* or Japanese miso can be used.

SERVES 2 × 2 TIMES

2 Asian eggplants
½ large onion
3 to 4 green onions (scallions)
1 teaspoon rapeseed or canola oil

A ingredients
Red chili pepper, to taste
Green chili pepper, to taste
1 tablespoon doenjang or miso
1 tablespoon each water, sake and mirin
1 teaspoon mulyeot (or honey)
1 teaspoon grated garlic
Freshly ground black pepper, to taste
1 teaspoon perilla oil

1 teaspoon roasted white sesame seeds

1 Cut the tops off the eggplants, and thinly slice lengthwise. Thinly slice the onion, and cut the green onions into 1½-in (3- to 4-cm) long pieces. Finely mince the red and green chili peppers for the A ingredient mixture.

2 Heat up a skillet over medium heat, and put in the eggplant slices. Pan-fry on both sides without adding oil, then remove from the skillet.

3 Heat up the rapeseed or canola oil in the skillet and stir-fry the onion slices. Add the combined A ingredients. Return the step-2 eggplant to the skillet and stir-fry quickly. Turn off the heat, add the green onions and sprinkle in the sesame seeds.

Spicy Konnyaku Stir-fry

Frying the konnyaku to gives it a plump texture. Tearing the konnyaku by hand instead of cutting it with a knife allows the flavors to soak in better.

SHELF LIFE — 3 to 4 days in the refrigerator

SERVES 2 × 2 TIMES

8 oz (250 g) konnyaku (devil's tongue jelly)
1 teaspoon rapeseed or canola oil
1 teaspoon sesame oil
½ tablespoon minced garlic

A ingredients

1 tablespoon mirin
½ tablespoon fish sauce
1 teaspoon ground chili pepper
1 teaspoon soy sauce

1 Briefly boil the konnyaku to remove its peculiar odor. Drain. Leave to cool, and then rip into small pieces with your hands. (Photo at right.)

2 Heat up the oils and the garlic in a skillet over low heat. When the garlic is fragrant, add the step-1 konnyaku and stir-fry.

3 Add the combined A ingredients, and stir-fry until there is no liquid left in the pan.

If you rip up the konnyaku, there will be more surface area on each piece, and the flavors will be better absorbed.

Konnyaku is a gelatinous Japanese food made from the root of the konjac plant. It is gray or translucent with a firm, rubbery texture and a neutral, slightly earthy taste. You can substitute shirataki noodles or dried tofu for konnyaku.

Sweet and Spicy Baby Anchovies with Nuts

Korean Nori and Rice Sushi Rolls

Sweet and Spicy Baby Anchovies with Nuts

SHELF LIFE: 5 to 6 days in the refrigerator

Stir-fried dried baby anchovies (*myeolchi*) are indispensable at the Korean dinner table. This crunchy combination with nuts makes for an irresistible treat. If you prefer it spicy, add a teaspoon or so of ground red chili pepper.

SERVES 2 × 2 TIMES

1 cup myeolchi (dried baby anchovies) (about 2 oz / 50 g)

A ingredients
- 1 tablespoon soy sauce
- 1 tablespoon mirin
- 1 tablespoon sugar

¼ cup unsalted nuts of your choice (about 1 oz / 30 g)
½ tablespoon mulyeot (or honey)
1 teaspoon roasted white sesame seeds

1 Dry-roast the baby anchovies in an unoiled skillet. Empty out into a fine meshed colander, and shake off the fine dust that comes off the fish.

2 Wipe out the skillet, add the combined A ingredients, and bring to a boil. Add the baby anchovies and nuts and stir-fry quickly, add the *mulyeot* (or honey) and mix. Sprinkle with the sesame seeds.

> **Myeolchi** have a strong, salty, umami flavor. You can substitute dried baby sardines or whitebait for myeolchi.

NOTE

Korean Nori and Rice Sushi Rolls

Kimbap or *gimbap*, Korean nori and rice rolls, made with Sweet and Spicy Baby Anchovies with Nuts is called "Myeolchi Kimbap." Here, I have combined them with just cucumber and perilla leaves, but I also recommend rolling them with omelet or takuan pickles.

1 Add the A ingredients to the hot rice and mix.
2 Put half the step-1 ingredients on one of the nori seaweed sheets and spread out thinly. Place a half sheet of nori seaweed on top and top with half each of the perilla leaves, cucumber and a portion of the Sweet and Spicy Baby Anchovies with Nuts. Roll up tightly. Roll up the remaining ingredients in the same way.
3 Brush a little sesame oil on the surface of the nori-wrapped rolls, sprinkle with salt and sesame seeds and slice into bite-size pieces.

SERVES 2 × 2 TIMES

A ingredients
- Pinch of salt
- 1 teaspoon sesame oil

2 portions hot cooked rice
3 whole sheets nori seaweed
4 perilla leaves
½ baby cucumber, thinly sliced
1 recipe Sweet and Spicy Baby Anchovies with Nuts
Sesame oil, for brushing
Salt, for sprinkling
Roasted white sesame seeds, for sprinkling

Stewed and Simmered Dishes

In addition to stewed meat and fish as main dishes, stewed tofu, beans and root vegetables are also a staple of banchan in South Korea. Whether made sweet and spicy, or spicy with gochujang or ground chili pepper, they are sure to make you want to eat more!

Simmered Chicken and Soybeans

SHELF LIFE: 4 to 5 days in the refrigerator

The plump soybeans absorb the umami of the chicken, making them delicious. The soy sauce and salt base gives this dish a light and mild flavor.

SERVES 2 × 2 TIMES

- 8 oz (250 g) boneless chicken thigh meat
- ½ tablespoon rapeseed or canola oil
- 4 cloves garlic, crushed

A ingredients
- ½ tablespoon sake
- 1 teaspoon soy sauce
- ¼ teaspoon salt
- Freshly ground black pepper, to taste

- ½ cup (90 g) boiled soybeans (➡ see below. Canned soybeans can be used instead)
- ¾ cup (185 ml) water
- Salt, to taste
- 1 teaspoon perilla oil
- 1 teaspoon perilla powder

1 Cut the chicken into bite-size pieces.
2 Heat up the rapeseed or canola oil and garlic in a skillet over medium heat. When the garlic is fragrant, add the step-1 cut-up chicken and cook on both sides. Add the A ingredients, the boiled soybeans and the water, and simmer for 20 minutes or so.
3 Season with additional salt, and add the perilla oil and perilla powder to finish.

To store, put the whole stew with cooking liquid in a container, cover with a lid, and refrigerate. To serve, heat in a microwave oven or transfer to a pan and return to a simmer.

NOTE

Boiled Soybeans

SHELF LIFE: 4 to 5 days in the refrigerator / 1 month in the freezer

In South Korea, soybeans are regarded as an ingredient that regulates one's health, and they are often stewed with meat or cooked with rice. When storing them, keep the soybeans soaking in the water used to boil them. Place them in a storage container, cover it with a lid, and place them in the refrigerator.

AN EASY-TO-MAKE AMOUNT (½ CUP)

1 Soak a scant ¼ cup of dried soybeans in plenty of water overnight.
2 Put the soybeans and water in a pan, and simmer over medium-low heat until tender, about 40 minutes.

Stewed and Simmered Dishes

Sweet and Spicy Chicken Drumettes

 SHELF LIFE 4 to 5 days in the refrigerator

The chicken and the vegetables are infused with the sweetness of the sauce. *Tteok* (Korean rice cakes) and potatoes can also be added.

SERVES 2 × 2 TIMES

8 chicken drumettes

A ingredients
Dash of salt and freshly ground black pepper
1 tablespoon sake

1 large onion (7 oz / 100 g)
1½ carrots (4 oz / 100 g)
1 teaspoon rapeseed or canola oil
3 cloves garlic, crushed

B ingredients
2 tablespoons gochujang
1 teaspoon ground chili pepper
1 teaspoon grated garlic
1 tablespoon soy sauce
1 tablespoon mulyeot (or honey)
⅓ cup, plus 4 teaspoons (100 ml) water

1 Cut a slit along the bone of each chicken drumette, and sprinkle with the A ingredients.
2 Cut the onion into ⅓-in (1-cm) wide dice, and roughly cut the carrot into small pieces.
3 Heat up the oil and garlic in a pan over medium heat. When the garlic is fragrant, add the step-1 chicken and stir-fry until browned. Add the step-2 vegetables and stir-fry. When all the ingredients are coated with oil, add the B ingredients, cover with a lid and simmer for about 30 minutes over medium heat.

Glazed Pork and Green Onion Rolls

SHELF LIFE — 5 days in the refrigerator

SERVES 2 × 2 TIMES

- 1 Japanese leek or large green onion (scallion)
- 5 perilla leaves
- 10 very thin slices pork cut for shabu shabu (5 oz / 150 g)
- Dashes of salt and freshly ground black pepper
- Flour, for dusting
- 1 teaspoon rapeseed or canola oil

A ingredients
- 2 tablespoons Gochujang Sauce (➡ page 52)
- 1 tablespoon sake

Try sprinkling with some roasted sesame seeds just before serving.

1 Cut the leek or green onion into 10 pieces (each about 1½-in / 4-cm long), and cut several diagonal slits into each piece. Remove the stems from the perilla leaves and cut them into halves lengthwise. Spread out the pork on a shallow tray or plate, and sprinkle with salt and black pepper.

2 Place a piece of perilla leaf and a piece of leek or green onion on top of a slice of pork (photo at right). Roll up the pork and dust with flour. Repeat with the rest of the pork, perilla and leek or green onion.

3 Heat up the oil in a skillet over medium heat, and place the step-2 rolls seam-side down in the pan. Fry on all sides while turning the rolls over occasionally.

4 Wipe out any excess oil in the pan, add the A ingredients and coat the rolls in it while simmering.

With the leek or green onion in the middle, roll up the pork and perilla leaf from the near end.

The sweetness of leek or green onion wrapped in pork and simmered in sweet and spicy sauce. It is perfect as a snack to nibble on with alcoholic drinks.

Stewed Meat-stuffed Eggplant

SHELF LIFE: 4 to 5 days in the refrigerator

Peeled and slow-cooked eggplant has a tender, fluffy texture. If stored with the broth, they keep their flavor well.

SERVES 2 × 2 TIMES

8 very small Asian eggplants
Flour, for dusting

A ingredients
1 tablespoon minced green onion (scallion)
1 teaspoon grated garlic
1 teaspoon soy sauce
1 teaspoon sesame oil
Salt and freshly ground black pepper

5 oz (150 g) ground pork

B ingredients
1¼ cups (300 ml) Dried Anchovy Dashi Stock (➡ page 4)
1 tablespoon mirin
1 teaspoon soy sauce
½ teaspoon salt

Green and red chili pepper, thinly sliced, to taste

1 Cut the tops off the eggplants, and peel them with a vegetable peeler.* Make crisscrossing cuts two thirds of the way into each eggplant from the bottom ends, and dust the insides with flour.

2 Add the A ingredients to the ground pork and mix. Divide into 8 portions and stuff into the step-1 eggplants (photo a, below). Compress lightly with your hands (photo b, below).

3 Put the B ingredients in a pan over medium heat, add the step-2 eggplants and simmer for about 20 minutes. When there is just a little liquid left in the pan, add the sliced chili peppers and turn off the heat.

a

Dust the insides of the eggplants before stuffing them so that the meat stuffing does not fall out.

b

Once you have stuffed the eggplants with meat, squeeze them lightly so that the meat sticks to the eggplant and to tidy up the shape.

*Use the peels to make namul (➡ page 35).

70 Side Dishes and Main Dishes

A favorite of Koreans, this dish is perfect as a main dish. Beef is boiled to remove any gaminess, and then simmered with eggs.

Beef and Eggs Simmered in Soy

SHELF LIFE: 4 to 5 days in the refrigerator

SERVES 2 × 2 TIMES

10 oz (330 g) beef round
20 quail eggs or 4 chicken eggs
Pinch of salt

A ingredients
- 2¼ cups (600 ml) water
- Vegetable scraps, such as the green tops and roots of green onions (scallions) or leeks, and onion skins
- ½ teaspoon whole black peppercorns
- 1 slice peeled fresh ginger

B ingredients
- 2 tablespoons soy sauce
- 1 tablespoon sugar
- Salt, to taste

4 cloves garlic
8 shishito peppers

1 Soak the beef in plenty of water for 20 minutes to eliminate the blood. Boil for 20 minutes, and then drain into a colander.

2 Boil the eggs for 3 to 4 minutes in water with a little salt added, cool and then peel.

3 Put the A ingredients in a pan over medium heat. Add the step-1 beef and cook for 30 to 40 minutes. Remove the beef, and strain the cooking liquid (there will be about 2 cups / 500 ml).

4 Return the cooking liquid to the pan, and mix in the B ingredients. Put the beef back in the pan and add the peeled eggs and garlic cloves. Cook for 20 minutes.

5 Take out the beef and shred it along the grain. Return the shredded beef to the pan. Add the shishito peppers and simmer for about 5 minutes.

Side Dishes and Main Dishes

Stewed Beef with Taro Root

 4 to 5 days in the refrigerator

SERVES 2 × 2 TIMES

A ingredients
- 1 teaspoon grated garlic
- 1 teaspoon soy sauce
- 1 teaspoon sugar
- Freshly ground black pepper, to taste
- 1 teaspoon sesame oil

- 7 oz (200 g) roughly chopped beef
- 8 small taro roots
- ½ Japanese leek or large green onion (scallion)
- 1 teaspoon rapeseed or canola oil

B ingredients
- ¾ cup, plus 1 tablespoon (200 ml) Dried Anchovy Dashi Stock (➡ page 4)
- 1 teaspoon soy sauce
- ⅓ teaspoon salt

- 2 tablespoons perilla powder

1 Rub the A ingredients into the beef. Peel the taro roots, and cut the leek or green onion into ⅓-in (1-cm) pieces.
2 Heat up the oil in a pan over medium heat, and stir-fry the beef. Add the taro root and Japanese leek or green onion and mix. Add the B ingredients and turn the heat down to low, and simmer while removing the scum until the taro roots are tender.
3 Mix a little of the cooking liquid with the perilla powder, add to the step-2 pan and mix.

The key is to thoroughly pre-season the beef. The perilla powder at the end adds flavor and richness.

Spicy Simmered Fish with Daikon Radish

 SHELF LIFE — 3 to 4 days in the refrigerator

A Korean way to cook fish is to spread radish, potatoes, onions, etc. in a pot, place the fish on top, and simmer. The tender flaky fish and the flavorful daikon radish are a treat.

SERVES 2 × 2 TIMES

- 4 pieces cutlassfish, mackerel or sea bass (about 10 oz / 330 g)
- Salt, for sprinkling
- 1½-in (4-cm) section daikon radish
- ⅓ Japanese leek or large green onion (scallion)

A ingredients
- ⅓ cup, plus 4 teaspoons (100 ml) Dried Anchovy Dashi Stock (➡ page 4)
- 1 tablespoon soy sauce
- 1 tablespoon mirin
- 1 tablespoon sake
- 1 teaspoon grated garlic
- 1 tablespoon or more ground chili pepper, to taste

1 Make a V-shaped cut into the back fin part of the fish and remove the fin. Sprinkle the fish with a little salt and leave for a few minutes. Pat dry with a paper towel. Cut the daikon radish section in half and slice into ⅓-in (1-cm) thick half-moon shapes. Thinly slice the leek or green onion diagonally.

2 Line a pan with the daikon radish slices, and add enough water to cover and heat over medium heat. Cook the daikon radish until a skewer goes through the pieces easily.

3 Discard the cooking liquid and top the daikon radish slices with the fish (photo at right). Add the A ingredients and simmer over medium heat for about 20 minutes. When the fish is cooked through, add the leek or green onion slices and simmer until there is just a little liquid left in the pan.

By lining the bottom of the pan with daikon radish, the fish won't get burnt or stuck to the pan, and you conveniently have a vegetable to eat on the side—so it's very efficient!

Cutlassfish are long, silver, ribbon-like fish found in warm coastal waters, especially around East Asia. They have soft, white flesh with a mild, slightly sweet flavor. You can substitute mackerel or sea bass for cutlassfish.

Put into a storage container and refrigerate. Reheat in the microwave before serving.

Stewed and Simmered Dishes

Spicy Spanish Mackerel Simmered with Potato

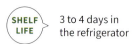

3 to 4 days in the refrigerator

This dish uses the same broth as in "Spicy Simmered Fish with Daikon Radish" (➡ page 75), but with different fish and vegetables. You can enjoy the soft, floury texture of potatoes. This can be made with cod instead of the Spanish mackerel.

SERVES 2 × 2 TIMES

4 pieces Spanish mackerel (or cod) (about 10 oz / 330 g)
Salt, for sprinkling
2 potatoes
⅓ Japanese leek or large green onion (scallion)

A ingredients
- ⅓ cup, plus 4 teaspoons (100 ml) Dried Anchovy Dashi Stock (➡ page 4)
- 1 tablespoon soy sauce
- 1 tablespoon mirin
- 1 tablespoon sake
- 1 teaspoon grated garlic
- 1 tablespoon or more ground chili pepper, to taste

1 Sprinkle the Spanish mackerel with a little salt and leave for a few minutes. Pat dry with a paper towel.
2 Peel the potatoes, cut them in half and slice the halves into ⅓-in (1-cm) thick half-moon shapes. Thinly slice the leek or green onion diagonally.
3 Line a pan with the potato slices and top with the step-1 fish. Add the A ingredients and simmer over medium heat for about 20 minutes. When the fish is cooked through, add the leek or green onion and simmer until there is just a little liquid left in the pan.

Korean Style Mackerel Simmered in Miso

SHELF LIFE: 3 to 4 days in the refrigerator

Utilize the miso pickling bed of Miso-based Jangajji for seasoning. Spread out the onion in the pan and simmer until it is meltingly soft.

SERVES 2 × 2 TIMES

4 pieces mackerel (about 10 oz / 330 g)
Salt, for sprinkling
1 onion
1 green chili pepper or shishito pepper

A ingredients

⅓ cup, plus 4 teaspoons (100 ml) Dried Anchovy Dashi Stock (➡ page 4)
3 tablespoons of the miso pickling bed of Miso Jangajji (➡ page 19)*
1 tablespoon mirin
1 tablespoon sake

* If using the miso bed after using it for marinating, add a little more than 3 tablespoons.

1 Sprinkle the mackerel with a little salt and leave for a few minutes. Pat dry with a paper towel.
2 Cut the onion in half, then cut the halves into ⅓-in (1-cm) wide slices. Slice the green chili pepper or shishito pepper into rounds.
3 Line the bottom of a pan with the onion slices and add the step-1 mackerel on top. Add the A ingredients and simmer for about 20 minutes until there is just a little liquid left in the pan.
4 Add the green chili pepper and turn off the heat.

Stewed and Simmered Dishes   77

Tofu Simmered with Kimchi

SHELF LIFE — About 2 days in the refrigerator

Kimchi is slowly stir-fried to concentrate the umami. Use mature pickled kimchi to utilize its sourness.

SERVES 2 × 2 TIMES

1 block firm tofu (about 10 oz / 330 g)
1 teaspoon sesame oil
1 scant cup (125 g) chopped napa cabbage kimchi

A ingredients

⅓ cup, plus 4 teaspoons (100 ml) Dried Anchovy Dashi Stock (➡ page 4)
1 teaspoon soy sauce
1 teaspoon mirin

Roasted white sesame seeds, for sprinkling

1 Wrap the tofu in paper towels and drain off the excess water. Cut into bite-size pieces.
2 Heat up the sesame oil in a skillet over medium-low heat. Add the kimchi and stir-fry slowly for about 2 minutes.
3 Add the fish and the A ingredients. Raise the temperature to medium and simmer for about 15 minutes. Sprinkle with sesame seeds.

> This is also delicious with fish filets, squid or pork added.

Tofu Simmered with Spicy Cod Roe

SHELF LIFE — About 2 days in the refrigerator

The tofu is covered with the umami and spiciness of the spicy preserved cod roe. Pan-fry the tofu before adding it to prevent it from falling apart.

SERVES 2 × 2 TIMES

1 block firm tofu (about 10 oz / 300 g)
Salt, for sprinkling
1 sac myeongran-jeot or mentaiko (spicy preserved pollock roe) (about 3¼ oz / 80 g)

A ingredients

4 tablespoons water
1 tablespoon mirin
1 teaspoon ground chili pepper
1 teaspoon sesame oil
⅓ teaspoon grated garlic

1 teaspoon rapeseed or canola oil
Green onion (scallion) (green parts), sliced, for serving (optional)

1 Wrap the tofu in paper towels to drain off the excess water. Cut into bite-size pieces. Sprinkle with salt to pre-season.
2 Remove the membrane from the spicy cod roe and mash up. Mix with the A ingredients
3 Heat up the rapeseed or canola oil in a skillet over medium heat. Pan-fry the step-1 tofu briefly on both sides. Add the step-2 ingredients and simmer until the spicy cod roe is cooked through.

> To serve, put the tofu on a serving dish and top with the spicy roe, and add some sliced green onion (if using).

> **Myeongran-jeot** (or *mentaiko*) is salted and fermented pollock roe. It appears as reddish, grainy sacs and has a salty, spicy and umami-rich flavor. You can substitute *tarako* (salted cod roe) for *myeongran-jeot* (or *mentaiko*).

Side Dishes and Main Dishes

Tofu Simmered with Kimchi

Tofu Simmered with Spicy Cod Roe

Stewed and Simmered Dishes

Spicy Fish Cakes with Onion

 SHELF LIFE About 5 days in the refrigerator

The sweetness of onions matches the umami of the *eumuk* (fried fish cakes). This is a standard Korean stew.

SERVES 2 × 2 TIMES

4 small eumuk or satsuma-age (deep-fried fish cakes) (about 4 oz / 100 g)
¼ onion
1 teaspoon rapeseed or canola oil

A ingredients
2 tablespoons water
1 tablespoon mirin
1 teaspoon ground chili pepper
1 teaspoon soy sauce
1 teaspoon mulyeot (or honey)
½ teaspoon grated garlic

Roasted white sesame seeds, for sprinkling

1 Thinly slice the fish cakes and onion.
2 Heat up the oil in a skillet over medium heat, and stir-fry the step-1 ingredients.
3 Add the A ingredients and simmer while stirring until there is no liquid left in the pan. Turn off the heat and sprinkle with sesame seeds.

Eumuk and **satsuma-age** are deep-fried fish cakes made from minced or pureed fish and seasonings. They have a chewy, slightly sweet, savory flavor.

80 Side Dishes and Main Dishes

Sweet and Spicy Boiled Eggs with Walnuts

Cook the eggs in a sweetened broth and throw in the walnuts. Boil the eggs to the desired degree of hardness. Up to 8 eggs can be cooked in the same amount of cooking liquid.

 SHELF LIFE: 3 to 4 days in the refrigerator

AN EASY-TO-MAKE AMOUNT

4–5 shelled walnuts (about 1 oz / 30 g)

A ingredients
- ¾ cup, plus 1 tablespoon (200 ml) Dried Anchovy Dashi Stock (➡ page 4)
- 1½ tablespoons soy sauce
- 1 tablespoon mirin
- ½ tablespoon mulyeot (or honey)
- ¼ teaspoon salt

4 to 8 boiled eggs

1 Soak the walnuts in plenty of boiling water for about 10 minutes. Drain.
2 Put the A ingredients in a pan over medium heat. Add the boiled eggs and simmer for about 10 minutes. If the cooking liquid does not cover the eggs, simmer while occasionally swirling the pan.
3 Add the step-1 walnuts to the pan. Coat them with the simmering liquid, and turn off the heat.

Seasoned Lotus Root

 About 5 days in the refrigerator

Stir-fry in oil and then slowly simmer. Finish with a sweetened sauce to increase the glossiness and richness.

SERVES 2 × 2 TIMES

7 oz (200 g) lotus root
1 teaspoon rapeseed or canola oil

A ingredients
- ⅓ cup, plus 4 teaspoons (100 ml) Dried Anchovy Dashi Stock (→ page 4)
- 1 tablespoon soy sauce
- 1 tablespoon sugar
- Pinch of salt
- ½ teaspoon grated garlic

B ingredients
- 1 tablespoon mulyeot (or honey)
- 1 teaspoon sesame oil

Roasted white sesame seeds, for serving (optional)

1. Peel the lotus root and cut it into scant ¼-in (5-mm) thick slices.
2. Add 1 teaspoon of vinegar (not included in the ingredients list) to a pan of boiling water, and boil the lotus root for 1 minute. Drain into a colander.
3. Heat up the rapeseed or canola oil in a skillet over medium heat, and stir-fry the boiled lotus root. When it is cooked through, add the A ingredients, turn the heat down to low and simmer until there is no liquid left in the pan.
4. Add the B ingredients, stir once and turn off the heat.

Sprinkle with some roasted white sesame seeds before serving, if using.

Potatoes Simmered with Dried Anchovies

 About 5 days in the refrigerator

The flavor of the broth infuses the potatoes.

SERVES 2 × 2 TIMES

3 potatoes (about 14 oz / 400 g)
¼ scant cup dried anchovies (myeolchi) (about ¼ oz / 10 g)
1 teaspoon rapeseed or canola oil
3 cloves garlic, crushed

A ingredients
- ¾ cup, plus 1 tablespoon (200 ml) water
- 1 tablespoon soy sauce
- 1 tablespoon mirin

1. Peel the potatoes and cut them into bite-size pieces.
2. Remove the heads and guts from the dried anchovies, and tear them in half lengthwise.
3. Heat up the oil in a skillet over medium heat, and stir-fry the garlic. When the garlic is fragrant, add the step-1 potatoes and stir-fry.
4. When the potatoes are coated with oil, add the step-2 anchovies and the A ingredients, and simmer for about 20 minutes, until the potatoes are tender.

Myeolchi are dried baby anchovies. They have a strong, salty, umami flavor. You can substitute dried baby sardines for *myeolchi*.

Stewed and Simmered Dishes 83

A Feast with a Cut of Meat

A cut of meat that can be prepared and divided into several portions is the centerpiece of a feast. These dishes are also great for entertaining.

Seasoned Boiled Pork

SHELF LIFE: 4 to 5 days in the refrigerator / about a month in the freezer

Boil together with the green tops of green onions and the stem and root ends of onions to remove any gamey taste from the meat. Eat wrapped in raw vegetables for a refreshing aftertaste.

AN EASY-TO-MAKE AMOUNT

1¼ lb (600 g) pork belly or pork shoulder

A ingredients
Vegetable scraps, such as the green tops of green onions (scallions) or leeks; the stem and root ends of onions and onion skins
1 teaspoon whole black peppercorns
3 cloves garlic
2 thin slices peeled fresh ginger
1 tablespoon doenjang or miso
3 dried jujubes
1 cinnamon stick (optional)

Saeujeot (fermented mysid shrimp preserved in salt), for serving
Miso pickling bed from Miso Jangajji (➡ page 19), for serving
Accompanying raw vegetables—lettuce, radicchio, perilla leaves, green chili peppers, garlic, etc.

1 Put the pork in a pan with 9 cups (2 liters) of water and the A ingredients over high heat.
2 When scum rises to the surface, skim it off and simmer the meat over medium heat for 40 to 50 minutes to cook it to the center. Turn off the heat, and leave the pork to cool in the cooking liquid.
3 When the meat has cooled down enough to handle, slice it into bite-size pieces, and arrange them on a serving platter with the accompanying vegetables. Serve with the saeujeot and miso pickling bed. Wrap in the vegetables to eat.

Place the sliced boiled pork in a storage container with the cooking liquid and refrigerate. If you store the pork with the vegetables from the A ingredients heaped on top, the sweetness of the vegetables will transfer to the meat and the surface will stay moist. If storing the meat in one piece, put it in a freezer storage bag together with the cooking liquid and the A-ingredients and freeze.

A Feast with a Cut of Meat

Pork Simmered with Asian Pear

SHELF LIFE 4 to 5 days in the refrigerator / about a month in the freezer

No water is added to this dish—the pork is cooked until tender with the juices and sweetness of the pears. Once cooked, the surface can be cooked in a skillet to a savory flavor. The cut of meat you use is up to you. I often make a combination of several kinds at once.

AN EASY-TO-MAKE AMOUNT

2 lbs (1 kg) pork shoulder, pork belly or pork leg

A ingredients

- 1 large Asian pear, skin-on and cut into wedges
- ⅓ Japanese leek or large green onion (scallion)
- 1 onion, cut into wedges
- 4 cloves garlic
- 4 dried jujubes
- 1 teaspoon whole black peppercorns
- Vegetable scraps, such as the roots of green onions and lotus root

Accompanying vegetables—zucchini, turnips, green beans etc.
Dash of salt and freshly ground black pepper

Sauce ingredients

- 4 tablespoons cooking liquid from this recipe
- 2 tablespoons soy sauce
- ½ teaspoon grated garlic
- Small portion minced green chili pepper, to taste

1 Poke the block of pork several times with a skewer to make it easier for the flavors to permeate.

2 Put the pork and the A ingredients in a heavy bottomed pan over medium heat (photo below). When it comes to a boil, turn the heat down to medium-low, and simmer for about 1 hour. Turn the meat over once during that time.

3 Slice the zucchini into rounds, and cut the turnips into quarters, leaving a little of the greens on. Pan-fry the vegetables in a skillet, and season with salt and pepper.

4 Cut up the step-2 meat into bite-size slices and arrange on a serving platter with the step-3 vegetables. Combine the Sauce ingredients together, and pour over everything.

Do not add water. The meat is simmered until tender in the juices expressed by the pear.

Place the sliced boiled pork in a storage container with the cooking liquid and refrigerate. If you store the pork with the vegetables and pear from the A ingredients heaped on top, the sweetness of the vegetables will transfer to the meat and the surface will stay moist. If storing the meat in one piece, put it in a freezer storage bag together with the cooking liquid and the A ingredients and freeze.

86 Side Dishes and Main Dishes

Jeon Pancakes

Jeon is a kind of savory pancake or pan-fried fritter. Meat, fish, vegetables or other ingredients are coated with batter and cooked in a skillet. It is an indispensable dish for *chuseok* (mid-fall harvest festival) and other memorial services. It is suitable for banchan because it is easy to make in advance.

Flour-based Jeon

SHELF LIFE: 4 to 5 days in the refrigerator for each type of jeon

Jeon can be served with soy sauce and vinegar, but Seasoned Soy Sauce (➡ page 15) works well. Onion Jangajji (➡ page 17) is also standard to serve with jeon, so please give it a try.

AN EASY-TO-MAKE AMOUNT

⅓ cup, plus 4 teaspoons (55 g) flour
2 tablespoons potato starch, cornstarch or mochi rice flour
⅓ cup, plus 4 teaspoons (100 ml) water

Combine the flour and starch or rice flour in a bowl. Add the water little by little until a thick, creamy batter is created.

> To reheat, warm the jeon on both sides in a skillet or in a toaster oven.

Corn and Onion Jeon

The crunchy texture and mild sweetness are excellent.

1 Scrape the kernels off an ear of corn with a knife. Chop ¼ an onion roughly.
2 Combine the step-1 ingredients in a bowl, add a heaping ⅓ cup (100 ml) of batter and mix.
3 Heat up 1 tablespoon of rapeseed or canola oil in a skillet over medium-low heat. Pour spoonfuls of the step-2 batter and vegetables into the pan and form into rounds. Pan-fry on both sides until lightly browned.

Napa Cabbage Jeon

Tear with your hands lengthwise along the rib and eat the stem along with the leaf.

1 Bash the stem parts of 6 small napa cabbage leaves to flatten them.
2 Coat both sides of each step-1 leaf with the batter on both sides.
3 Heat up 1 tablespoon of rapeseed or canola oil in a skillet over medium-low heat. Add the step-2 fritters and pan-fry on both sides until a little browned.

Shrimp and Chrysanthemum Greens Jeon

The umami of the shrimp really contrasts well with the fragrance of the chrysanthemum greens.

1 Prepare 2 cups (4 oz / 100 g) of roughly chopped chrysanthemum greens, and mix with a heaping ⅓ cup (100 ml) of batter.
2 Heat up 1 tablespoon of rapeseed or canola oil in a skillet over medium-low heat. Add spoonfuls of step-1 batter and make 8 small fritters.
3 Place a peeled shrimp on each fritter, and pan-fry the fritter on both sides until lightly browned.

Flour-based Jeon

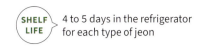 4 to 5 days in the refrigerator for each type of jeon

Beet and Onion Jeon

Make these jeon with colorful, nutrition-packed beets. The sticky texture is unexpected!

1 Peel one small beet and thinly slice it. Thinly slice ¼ onion.
2 Combine the step-1 ingredients in a bowl, and add a heaping ⅓ cup (100 ml) of batter. Mix well.
3 Heat up ½ tablespoon of rapeseed or canola oil in a skillet over medium-low heat. Add spoonfuls of the step-2 mixture and form into rounds. Pan-fry on both sides until lightly browned.

Arugula Jeon

Pan-fry the fritters, preserving the shape of the leaves, and enjoy the slightly bitter flavor.

1 Dip 2½ cups of loosely packed arugula leaves (about 2 oz / 50 g) one by one into the batter.
2 Heat up ½ tablespoon of rapeseed or canola oil in a skillet over medium-low heat. Add the step-1 batter-coated leaves and pan-fry until a little browned on both sides.

Whitebait and Green Onion Jeon

Umami, saltiness and bitterness come together with the batter. Pan-fry to a refreshing color.

1 Put ⅓ cup (about 3½ oz / 85 g) of salted whitebait and a similar volume of minced green onion (scallion) in a bowl. Add a heaping ⅓ cup (100 ml) of batter and mix well.
2 Heat up 1 tablespoon rapeseed or canola oil in an 8-in (20-cm) diameter skillet over medium-low heat and add the step-1 ingredients. Pan-fry the fritter on both sides until lightly browned, and slice into bite-size pieces.

Jeon Pancakes 91

Nori Wrapped Enoki Jeon

Wrap enoki mushrooms with nori seaweed to make them easier to eat. The egg-based batter tastes very mellow.

 SHELF LIFE 2 to 3 days in the refrigerator

AN EASY-TO-MAKE AMOUNT

1 egg
Dash of little salt
1 sheet nori seaweed
1 bunch enoki mushrooms (about 4 oz /100 g)
1 tablespoon rapeseed or canola oil

Serve with a little Seasoned Soy Sauce (➡ page 15) on the side.

1 Break the egg into a bowl and beat it. Add the salt and mix to make the batter.

2 Cut the nori seaweed into $\frac{1}{3}$ × $2\frac{1}{3}$-in (1 × 6-cm) strips.

Wrap bite-size bundles of enoki mushrooms with nori seaweed, and secure the ends with water.

3 Cut the bases off of the enoki mushrooms and divide the cluster into easy-to-eat clumps. Wrap each bundle with a nori strip (photo at left). Secure the end of each nori strip with a dab of water.

4 Heat up the oil in a skillet over medium-low heat. Dip the step-2 bundles in the step-1 batter and arrange in the skillet. Pan-fry until light brown on both sides.

Side Dishes and Main Dishes

Rice Jeon

SHELF LIFE: 2 to 3 days in the refrigerator

A lightly flavored jeon with whisked egg whites as batter. They can be made with leftover rice and vegetables. The button mushrooms can be replaced with shiitake or shimeji mushrooms.

AN EASY-TO-MAKE AMOUNT

1 egg white
¾ cup cooked rice (about 5 oz / 150 g)

A ingredients

3 tablespoons minced onion
1 tablespoon minced button mushrooms
Pinch of salt
Pinch of freshly ground black pepper

1 tablespoon rapeseed or canola oil

1 Put the egg white in a bowl and whisk until white and foamy.
2 In a separate bowl, combine the rice and the A ingredients. Add the step-1 egg white and mix.
3 Heat up the oil in a skillet over medium-low heat. Add spoonfuls of the step-2 mixture and form round fritters. Pan-fry on both sides until lightly browned.

Jeon Pancakes   93

Shredded Sweet Potato Jeon

  SHELF LIFE: 2 to 3 days in the refrigerator

The natural sweetness of sweet potatoes makes this jeon a great snack. Putting the shredded sweet potato in water beforehand makes the fritters crispy when cooked.

AN EASY-TO-MAKE AMOUNT

1 sweet potato (about 5 oz / 150 g)

A ingredients
- 1 tablespoon flour
- 1 tablespoon potato starch or cornstarch
- Dash of salt and freshly ground black pepper

1 tablespoon rapeseed or canola oil

1 Wash the sweet potato well and shred it with the skin on. Soak in a bowl of cold water for 2 minutes to rinse away the surface starch.

2 Drain into a colander, put into a bowl, add the A ingredients, and mix.

3 Heat up the oil in a skillet over medium-low heat. Add spoonfuls of the step-2 mixture. Pan-fry until lightly browned on both sides.

These are also delicious if you add some shredded cheese to the fritters before reheating them. The jeon can be made with potato instead of sweet potato.

Side Dishes and Main Dishes

Stuffed Shiitake Jeon

SHELF LIFE: 2 to 3 days in the refrigerator

The soft meat filling with tofu goes well with shiitake mushrooms. If you have leftover meat stuffing, batter and pan-fry them in the same way to turn them into jeon.

MAKES 8

8 small fresh shiitake mushrooms
1 tablespoon flour
1 beaten egg

A ingredients

4 oz (100 g) ground beef
¼ block (3 oz / 75 g) firm tofu
2 tablespoons minced green onion (scallion)
1 teaspoon grated garlic
1 teaspoon sesame oil
½ teaspoon soy sauce
¼ teaspoon salt
Pinch of freshly ground black pepper

1 tablespoon rapeseed or canola oil

1 Cut the stems off the mushrooms, cut 5 small slits on the top sides of the caps, and dust the bottom sides of the caps with flour.
2 Put the A ingredients in a bowl and mix together well. Divide into 8 equal portions and stuff inside the mushroom caps. Dust with the remaining flour, and brush with the beaten egg.
3 Heat up the oil in a skillet over medium-low heat. Place the mushrooms meat-side down in the pan. Cook for about 3 minutes, turn over, and cook until done on the other side.

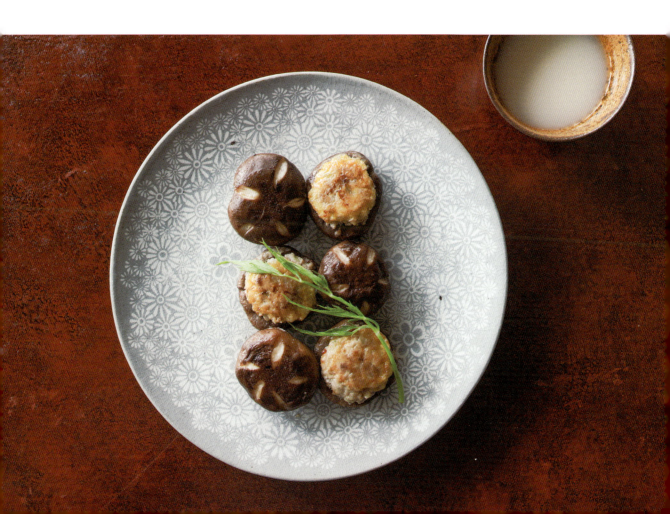

"Books to Span the East and West"

Tuttle Publishing was founded in 1832 in the small New England town of Rutland, Vermont [USA]. Our core values remain as strong today as they were then—to publish best-in-class books which bring people together one page at a time. In 1948, we established a publishing outpost in Japan—and Tuttle is now a leader in publishing English-language books about the arts, languages and cultures of Asia. The world has become a much smaller place today and Asia's economic and cultural influence has grown. Yet the need for meaningful dialogue and information about this diverse region has never been greater. Over the past seven decades, Tuttle has published thousands of books on subjects ranging from martial arts and paper crafts to language learning and literature—and our talented authors, illustrators, designers and photographers have won many prestigious awards. We welcome you to explore the wealth of information available on Asia at **www.tuttlepublishing.com**.

Published by Tuttle Publishing, an imprint of Periplus Editions (HK) Ltd.

www.tuttlepublishing.com

ISBN 978-0-8048-5810-6

Mippanchan: Mainichi no Gohan Zukuri ga Raku ni Naru Kankoku no Jobisai 100
Copyright © Nobuko Kitasaka 2023
English translation rights arranged with
Shufu-to-Seikatsusha, Ltd. through
Japan UNI Agency, Inc., Tokyo

All rights reserved. The items (text, photographs, drawings, etc.) included in this book are solely for personal use, and may not be reproduced for commercial purposes without permission of the copyright holders.

English translation © 2025 Periplus Editions (HK) Ltd.
Translated from Japanese by Makiko Itoh

Distributed by:
North America, Latin America & Europe
Tuttle Publishing
364 Innovation Drive
North Clarendon
VT 05759-9436 U.S.A.
Tel: (802) 773-8930 | Fax: (802) 773-6993
info@tuttlepublishing.com
www.tuttlepublishing.com

Asia Pacific
Berkeley Books Pte. Ltd.
3 Kallang Sector, #04-01
Singapore 349278
Tel: (65) 6741-2178 | Fax: (65) 6741-2179
inquiries@periplus.com.sg
www.tuttlepublishing.com

GPSR representative
Matt Parsons
matt.parsons@upi2mbooks.hr
UPI-2M PLUS d.o.o., Medulićeva 20,
10000 Zagreb, Croatia

29 28 27 26 25   10 9 8 7 6 5 4 3 2 1
Printed in China   2507EP

TUTTLE PUBLISHING® is a registered trademark of Tuttle Publishing, a division of Periplus Editions (HK) Ltd.